Teaching Struggling Readers to Make Sense of What They Read

NOW I GET IT!

Joan Lazar & Christine Vogel

SCHOLASTIC

New York • Toronto • London • Auckland • Sydney
Mexico City • New Delhi • Hong Kong • Buenos Aires

Dedication:

To our mothers and sisters and all the strong women in our lives who have loved us, supported us, and shown us the way.

Editor: Lois Bridges

Production management: Amy Rowe

Cover design: Brian LaRossa

Interior design: Holly Grundon

Copy editor: Eileen Judge

ISBN-13: 978-0-545-10583-5

ISBN-10: 0-545-10583-8

Copyright © 2010 by Joan Lazar and Christine Vogel

Table of Contents

Acknowledgments

The authors of this book met early in their careers in formal education, working together at an alternative school in Newark, New Jersey, and have continued to work collaboratively, teaching reading and writing to people of disparate ages and abilities. As Joan is currently working as a reading specialist and classroom teacher, we have, in the body of the book, written in Joan's voice in the first person singular and used examples from Joan's classroom and students. In reading these acknowledgments, you will note that some are joint and some are individual.

First, we want to acknowledge the people whose seminal miscue research and powerful insights are the foundation of this book and were the basis for our successful work in teaching reading and writing with learners of all ages: Kenneth Goodman, Yetta Goodman, Dorothy Menosky, Dorothy Watson, Carolyn Burke, Jerome Harste, Bess Altwerger, and Frank Smith.

We want, also, to acknowledge the people, grant-makers, and organizations that supported our experimental work in Newark, New Jersey, which enabled us to develop and flesh out effective instructional procedures for children, teenagers, and adults: Dorothy Menosky, who was our consultant for many years; the faculty, staff, and students of The Learning Experience Alternative High School, where Christine was the founding principal and Joan the reading specialist; the Sisters of St. Joseph of Peace, The Fund for New Jersey, the Geraldine R. Dodge Foundation, the Victoria Foundation, the Ford Foundation, and the Prudential Foundation for their early and enduring belief in our work and for their financial support of its development at The Learning Experience, Reading Naturally, and The Newark Literacy Campaign.

Each book is written because of the efforts of many people who contribute in some way to its making. So, too, with this book, thanks are due to many people: Erika Thulin-Dawes, who first encouraged us to write the book; Bess Altwerger, whose continuing support and wise counsel made it possible for us to structure the book usefully for teachers; Dorothy Cantor, who provided many creative ideas for communicating with teachers and parents; our talented and encouraging editor at Scholastic, Lois Bridges, who helped us shape our ideas into a publishable book concept and guided it into its present format, and our supportive production manager, Amy Rowe, who with her talented design and production team, produced the book you are about to read.

Finally we would like to thank fellow educators we have worked with and been supported by throughout our careers. For Joan: my first Teaneck principal, Elise Bourne-Busby, whose enthusiastic encouragement and interest propelled me to continue writing; my Livingston, New Jersey, Language Arts Supervisor, Bobbi Fredrickson, whose unflinching belief in me came at a crucial time; my Literacy Coach partner at Hawthorne School in Teaneck, New Jersey, Janet Bus, who always has such good ideas; my Teaneck, New Jersey, Language Arts Supervisor, Deirdre Spollen-La Raia; and Principal Vincent McHale, whose ongoing feedback has helped me to improve my work in the classroom and, thus, the effectiveness of this book. For Christine: my mother Virginia Vogel McLeod—the best writer I know—for being a role model in so many ways, both personally and professionally; my teachers Sister Irene Marie, O. P., at Lacordaire Academy, and Dr. Robert W. Ayers of the English Department at Georgetown University; and the entire faculty of St. Vincent Academy in Newark, New Jersey, especially Sister June Favata. Collectively, you taught me what being a teacher is all about.

Introduction

Facilitating Breakthroughs for Struggling Readers

The short chapters in this book alternate between direct comments to you, the teacher, and collections of classroom-tested lessons designed to help students sharpen their use of language and logic in order to understand more and more of what they are reading. The good news is that the lessons work! The better news is that students enjoy them and develop skills that can be applied at ever-increasing levels of reading difficulty.

Engaging students in these lessons quickly leads to breakthroughs. Students in my classroom have, on more than one occasion, expressed their surprise at their own achievements by exclaiming, "Now I get it!" I usually interpret that to mean, "Why didn't anyone ever tell me this was what I was supposed to be doing all along?"

The lessons contained herein have changed the lives of thousands of young people. I have seen students who, like me, were so defeated by what they viewed as their own failure to learn to read that they would not even try anymore. In fact, some would not even open a book. In just one session, that bleak attitude can begin to dissolve as your student sees that, with the application of a little bit of logic and her own good sense, she can understand what the author is talking about. The first thing that happens is that the student sits up straighter and is clearly ready for more. The next step is to apply what has been learned to reading something the student wants to be able to understand. It may be the sports page of the newspaper, a textbook from another class, or a library book she has been carrying around but hasn't been able to master.

A Reading Strategy Is a Reading Decision

All people who read written language employ reading strategies. Some people use efficient and effective reading strategies because they have found that these strategies aid them in making sense of written language—no matter how difficult the text might be. I remember spending the better part of a month trying to interpret the very first paragraph of a *Scientific American* article about nuclear physics, entitled "The Eight-Fold Way." I knew in my heart that if I could just understand the first paragraph clearly, I would be able to understand much of the rest of the article (which, in fact, I was eventually able to do). At that time in my life, I wanted very much to understand the concept of weak and strong nuclear forces. My process was to test out my predictions about what each phrase in the first paragraph might mean using all of the strategies described and recommended in this book.

When I was much younger, however, I had embraced an entirely different kind of process while reading that did not help me understand much of what I read. My goal at that time was to try to name precisely every single word I saw. Meaning took a backseat to naming words. So my reading strategies were to sound out, spell out, and try to recall every unfamiliar word. And I would keep doing that no matter what. These reading strategies were ineffective and inefficient because they resulted in my never reading a book until the fifth grade. I could not stand the feeling of not knowing every single word on each page. My decision, as a young learner to use every trick I knew to name the words, changed as I grew up. In later years, when I became interested in learning subject matter, I began to use every trick I could figure out to understand the authors better. As an adult, I adopted more effective and efficient reading strategies to help attain my goal of making sense of written language, no matter how difficult that might be. The reading strategy lessons you will be using show learners the kinds of reading decisions that proficient readers make rapidly and automatically in order to understand the author. When readers use these strategies often enough in a conscious and deliberate way, at some point, the practices become unconscious skills that they apply automatically whenever they read.

This book does not contain a lot of theory; instead it focuses on practical "how-to" instructions and provides sample lessons of increasing difficulty that demonstrate the successful approach I have developed to using such lessons to help students gain a greater understanding of what they are reading. At the end of each chapter, you'll find a "Frequently Asked Questions" section that addresses the questions I am often asked by the teachers I train.

Which Reading Strategy Lesson Should I Teach First?

One of the most common of those questions is, "Which strategy lesson should I teach first?" The best answer to that question is to use the strategy that responds to the problem the student reader is encountering, and to use it at the moment it will be most useful—during the student's struggle for meaning. This means that as you become familiar with the circumstances (described in conjunction with the reading strategy that addresses those circumstances), you will learn to diagnose just what the problem is that your student is experiencing and to identify the strategy that will provide the most help for that reader.

There is, however, somewhat of a hierarchical order to the strategies. It is possible to teach the strategies in order, and I have presented them in this book in that order. However, I do want to stress, once again, that these same strategies should be taught over and over again as students engage with print at increasing levels of difficulty; and a strategy used at a "teachable moment" is more likely to accelerate the reader's development in his search for sensible meaning from print.

The Reading Strategies

People learn reading strategies most easily when they are trying to understand material that they care about. Maybe they want to understand the class textbook. Maybe they want to understand a guided reading book about snakes. Most of the time, the learners want to read materials that also feel comfortable to them. I sometimes call these materials "at the reader's level," which means that the reader has a lot of prior knowledge of both the content and the language used in the material. I can also say these materials are at the reader's "comfort level." However, sometimes people want to read material that is not at their comfort level. Sometimes people want to research specific information on the Web, and the Web site is not written at the reader's comfort level—far from it. The English is denser than the reader is used to, or perhaps the reader has only some prior knowledge of the topics and concepts presented on the Web page. In that case, I might say the reader is trying to understand material that is at a "discomfort level." Readers sometimes describe materials that are at an uncomfortable level as being a little "advanced" for them.

Strategies for Readers at Beginning Levels

These four reading strategy lessons are used with books at the readers' levels, both in terms of concept and language—books that they would understand very well if the books were read to them:

- **Cloze**—helps readers deal with words they do not know.

- **Nicknaming**—invites learners to name each unfamiliar proper noun by its first letter as they work to figure out its function in the text.

- **Scattered Clues**—the most powerful of the strategies; creates a precise model of the reading process, teaching readers to make logical predictions and to constantly re-evaluate and adjust those predictions against the criteria of new information gathered from the text.

- **Paraphrasing**—putting what you have read in your own words; used in combination with all of the strategies presented in this book.

Strategies for Readers at More Advanced Levels

These more advanced reading strategy lessons are used with students who are reading materials that are either conceptually or linguistically beyond their reading level—text contained in materials like textbooks, scholarly journals, reference books, standardized reading tests, and some Web sites.

- **Nonsense**—answers the question, "What do I do when I only know very few of the words I am trying to read?"

- **Referents**—helps readers keep track of the meaning of longer and more complicated sentences by helping them identify to whom or to what pronouns refer.

- **Unraveling**—teaches students the tricks of sentence-combining and how to reverse the process to take apart complex sentences into their several simpler ideas.

- **Kerneling**—involves eliminating all but the essential elements (subject, verb, direct object) when trying to understand very challenging material.

How Do I Know Which Strategy Lesson to Use to Help My Struggling Readers Break Through to Increased Comprehension?

In order to know which strategy lesson might be the most useful to improve a student's reading comprehension, you should pay careful attention to the student's oral reading pattern and his retelling of those books he would be able to understand if they were read to him. At the beginning of each chapter, I provide an example of real a problem encountered by one of my students to help you recognize the same problem when experienced by your own students. I then provide a description of the reading strategy that you can teach your students to use to replace the current ineffective reading strategy.

After the explanation of the reading strategy and how to teach it, there follows a number of sample strategy lessons you can use. There are also instructions for making your own strategy lessons from the texts your students are reading or from other texts on subjects of interest to your students. Making your own strategy lessons will enable you to have as many lessons as you need on topics of interest and at the appropriate levels to challenge your learners to become more proficient readers.

The Irrefutable Logic of Results

In the following pages, I am going to walk you through a simple but theoretically grounded approach to helping all readers improve their reading comprehension by developing their logic skills and learning how to approach reading content. I will introduce you to a group of practical strategies that guide readers along the road to reading mastery. This approach and these strategies have proven to be effective with individual students, as well as small and large groups; with learners from second graders through adults; in classrooms of all subjects and reading labs, as well as in living rooms and kitchens; and when presented by teachers, coaches, tutors, parents, aunts, uncles, grandparents, cousins, and older brothers and sisters. It is an approach, not a method—although I provide step-by-step examples of the approach in action—so it can be shaped by the teacher of any subject to work in the situation at hand.

Throughout this book, I will share my stories and those of some of my students. I have, of course, changed the names of my students, but their stories and their struggles are quite real. I will explain how to apply the very simple techniques and exercises I use to help readers improve their logic skills and apply their own good common sense to the process of improving their reading comprehension. If you have the patience to develop some new ideas, and if I have the skill to explain these lessons clearly, soon we will be helping tens of thousands of readers escape from the terror of struggling with reading as they improve their reading comprehension.

What I Believe About Reading
and How I Came to Believe It

It was a rainy day in October. My mother, a gifted elementary school teacher, rarely showed the strain of dealing with 10-year-old me, but today, she was clearly at her wits' end. As I neared the familiar building in Sheepshead Bay, I began to walk more slowly, as I always did, and she asked me to come inside with her, as she always did. I refused to go with her, stating firmly that I would wait outside. For almost ten minutes, she cajoled, bargained, even insisted, but to no avail. The last place on earth I would willingly go to was a public library.

I was not uninterested in books; I was terrified of them. The reason was simple—at 10 years old, I thought that reading was too hard for me. Oh, I knew many words by sight, but there were other words I didn't know, and I didn't know what to do when they popped up in what I was trying to read. All I could think of was what I didn't know. I thought I had to know every word and when I didn't, I just gave up. I felt that if I didn't know all the words, I had no right to read the book. Those unknown words terrified me so much that I couldn't even use what I did know to figure out the meaning of what I was trying to read.

After having been pronounced an academic failure by my fifth-grade teacher, who suggested that special education might be the best solution for my particular problems, I had the good luck to contract the chicken pox. Desperate for entertainment, among the books in my room I found one that captured my interest. It was a book about a heroic Saint Bernard who rescued people buried in snow. It was completely exciting from the first paragraph onward. There were few helpful pictures. I can recall wondering what a Saint Bernard was and getting a little bit scared about not knowing. But as I was compelled to read on, I soon realized it was a really big, strong dog. I recall skipping quickly over two unfamiliar words at the bottom of the first page in order to turn the page over to see what the dog was going to do. It was only after I had turned the page and read on that it dawned on me what those words probably meant. I recall going back to them, noticing their letters and asking myself what words do I know that look like "that" and mean "this." By combining the meaning I had surmised with my knowledge of phonetics, I was able to recognize both words precisely. (Fortunately, I had a good listening vocabulary and so could use meaning and phonetics fairly frequently to figure out the precise words I had skipped.)

Little did I know at the time that my own educational development was preparing me for the day, years later, when I would first hear the theory of psycholinguistics and come to understand the definition of reading as a search by the reader for sensible meaning, using his own experience and his knowledge of language to provide clues to the author's possible meaning. Little did I realize at the time that hearing a college professor describe my own experience with struggling to read would change my life.

My other personal educational epiphany occurred when I was in the seventh grade. It was during that year that I became carried away by my interest in science. I was completely captivated by it and tried to learn everything I could about it for the next ten years. Nothing could stop me and nothing could satisfy my thirst for learning. In fact, this "slow learner" who had been in the lowest academic section in the seventh grade was pursuing an advanced degree in chemistry at Yale on full scholarship when I finally put on the brakes and looped back to face the problem I had been avoiding all my life.

At Yale, I found that my curiosity about chemistry had been sated. I discovered I had no talent for work in the lab, and I began to yearn to make a contribution, to do something that would help other people in a direct way. Was it any wonder I began to try to help other people to learn how to read? I still love science. I think that is what drives me to continue to work on understanding the reading process more precisely. I view the work I have been doing in the classroom as trying to understand the reading process scientifically so that I can invent effective and efficient instruction for learners.

Finding the Words to Explain How Reading Works

At first, I was not able to explain my own reading breakthrough to others in a way that enabled them to benefit from my experience. I needed a framework for helping poor readers learn how to become good readers. I needed a theory and methods to provide structure and depth to my work in teaching reading.

It was for that reason, that on another rainy October evening, I found myself taking one last stab at meeting these needs in an institution of higher education. I had started to take classes in reading theory and instruction, but none of what was being said to me was consistent with my own experience of how I, with that dog's help, had taught myself to read back when I had the chicken pox. I was ready to quit graduate school—again—when a friend said, "Come hear my professor tonight before you give up. She really makes a lot of sense to me." I didn't expect much, but I felt at that point I had nothing to lose, so I went.

I shall never forget the first time I heard Dr. Dorothy Menosky speak about reading as the active search for sensible meaning. What a concept! I wanted to know more. Dr. Menosky explained that reading is a psycholinguistic process of prediction and inference. That took some digesting. What she was saying was that each of us knows a certain amount about any given thing (psycho) and that we all have a certain level of development in the use and appreciation of language (linguistic). In reading, we are asked to apply what we know about the subject and what we know about the English language to predict the author's meaning, and then confirm or dispute the correctness of our prediction, as we read on, forming new hypotheses—or ideas about what the meaning might be—as we are presented with information that seems to contradict our original hypothesis, or idea. In this way, good readers self-correct as they continue to read what the author has written.

For example, when children try to understand a story about Encyclopedia Brown, a well-known fictional child detective, they first think they are reading about a book—an encyclopedia. But when they read that Encyclopedia Brown loves chocolate, well, something is not making sense here and only the better readers, and thinkers, realize it. Then a girl gives Encyclopedia a quarter to help her find out who took her sneaker. Now they are pretty sure that Encyclopedia Brown is a person who might help this girl solve a mystery. As the clues about Encyclopedia Brown continue to add up, the attentive reader will figure out who and what he is. However, the struggling reader may remain upset by the unfamiliar word *Encyclopedia* or by its unusual use in this story.

Dr. Menosky went on to explain that when we are first learning about a new subject, we have to build up a conceptual vocabulary. This suggests that we should read books about new subject matter that are written in language and with a style that is comfortable for us. If we are reading about a subject with which we are more familiar, about which our knowledge is more sophisticated, we can deal with material written in a style that challenges our language ability.

Balancing Understanding of Concepts and Language to Support the Search for Meaning in Print

Let me explain this the way a friend of mine, a high school English teacher, does. If her students are reading a play by Shakespeare, she tells them what happens in the story before they read the scene. That's because they are all familiar with the basic emotional conflicts and the types of struggles that go on in Shakespeare's plays. Once the students are confident that they know what they are reading about, they can pay more attention to the way these things are written. The style and form of the writing are new to them. If, however, the students are reading the papers of their classmates, whose language abilities are about on a par with their own, the focus is on the meaning of what their classmates have written.

Although she has a master's degree in teaching, my friend often buys picture books about subjects in which she is developing an interest. She knows that by understanding some basic concepts about a subject, she is preparing herself to read and understand more advanced books on the topic. She knows that her own reading level varies based on her familiarity with both the subject matter and the language style of the reading material.

My Career Helping Readers Make Breakthroughs in Comprehension

Dr. Menosky's explanation, addressing so many of the hitherto unanswered questions that had plagued me, kept me in school and sustained me as I began a career teaching reading and becoming a reading specialist—helping students having difficulty learning to read well and training others to teach reading. In the years since that lecture, I have developed an approach to teaching reading at a private alternative high school in Newark, New Jersey; I founded and directed the Newark Literacy Campaign, which is still training adults to tutor readers from age 9 to adult, and providing tutoring services from the Newark Public Library. I have also had the joy of working with elementary and middle school students and their teachers in both inner city and suburban public school districts.

As I see it, if one has not achieved comprehension—the ability to put what one has read into one's own words and explain it to someone else—one is not reading, but rather simply pronouncing. *Reading* in this book means understanding. *Reading* in this book will never mean "saying the words," or "pronouncing the words," or "saying the words aloud." When I speak of learners reading successfully, I mean that they have understood the authors as well as they are able given their prior knowledge—they get it!

Replacing Fear With Joy

It was only after I had discovered for myself—although at the time I didn't have the words to describe it this way—that reading is the active search for sensible meaning, that reading is a psycholinguistic process of prediction and inference, that I didn't always have to know the meaning of every word on every page to comprehend what I was reading, that the fear of reading left me and a new joy came into my life: the joy of reading. It is a joy that has grown with every book I have devoured since that time. It is a joy that I have dedicated my life to spreading, first as a high school teacher, then as the founder and director of a literacy program for adults, and now, saving the best for last, as the teacher of upper elementary school students who are on the verge of becoming readers or non-readers for the rest of their lives. If they are willing, I help them choose to become readers. Through this book, I hope to help many young people I will never meet by helping their teachers engage them in enjoyable lessons designed to help them sharpen their logic skills and apply them along with their own experience and common sense to understanding what authors mean.

Meeting the Comprehension Crisis of Grade 3 Head-On

Why do many students experience a crisis in their reading comprehension during the third grade and beyond? To comprehend what authors have written, good readers approach reading as a search for sensible meaning. They are not satisfied merely to pronounce the words; instead, they form hypotheses about the meaning of the author's words, and they check those hypotheses against additional information they gather by reading further. Good readers do three other mental activities constantly as they read:

1. Reflect upon their prior knowledge of both language and content

2. Employ logic

3. Reflect upon and scour the context for helpful clues to clarify the author's meaning

Developing readers do not do these things, or do them to a lesser extent, resulting in a crisis of comprehension as both language and concepts become more complex. If this crisis of comprehension is not confronted when it first begins to develop, it becomes the comprehension crisis of grades 4, 5, 6, 12, and—until it is addressed and a reading comprehension breakthrough is made by the reader.

Most struggling fourth-grade readers I have encountered at the elementary school in New Jersey where I have taught for the past three years have normally been intelligent, fluent readers, with very poor reading comprehension when they began in my class. Almost every child could pronounce accurately 98 percent of the text of the guided reading books. Many children were 100 percent accurate and even said the sentences with lots of expression. Yet, when these children were asked to explain the meaning of the story, or paragraph, or sentence they had just said aloud, they were not able to explain even the most basic information. Most of the children could say the words they saw, but did not understand what they were "reading." In some ways, being able to pronounce all the words might, in a strange way, be viewed as an impediment to the students' understanding, in that they may comprehend almost nothing while they pronounce all the words correctly.

If teachers buy into the notion that good reading is good pronouncing, the result can be damaging to the child. This is because a child who hears "He reads well, but has trouble with comprehension" may focus on the first part and dismiss the second. If teachers test children's reading ability only by asking them to read bits of text aloud and never ask the children what it means to them, that reinforces the idea that the way to win the game is to be able to pronounce the words correctly and quickly. When he can pronounce the words in this manner, the child, also, believes he is a good reader and doesn't worry about his inability to understand the meaning, since no one else seems to be focused on that. It is critically important that if a child can pronounce but not understand, the teacher recognizes and the student does, too, that he is not reading well. This book offers teachers an enjoyable approach to turning that situation around rapidly.

Giving Students the Tools to Tackle Text

My approach involves explicit teaching—showing children how text works and how they can work to make sense of text. It builds on students' knowledge—showing them how they can use their knowledge and experiences in the world to make sense of text. It helps students view themselves as successful readers and writers—increasing their confidence as they begin to see their own agency in actively constructing meaning from text.

Developing readers are those who understand less than they are capable of understanding. This is demonstrated by the fact that when they are read to and do not look at the page, they understand far more of the material than when they read it to themselves. In this book I will talk about how to determine whether your student is a developing reader. I will also share a whole tool kit of practical strategies and techniques for helping that student become a better reader.

What works in both teachers' and students' favor is that from mid–second grade onward, struggling readers want to know how adults often seem able to understand what they read when faced with complicated material. Struggling readers become alert and ready to throw off their ineffective reading strategies in order to learn to read like the adults around them in school.

In my work with elementary and high school students, in the very first instructional session students realize that they can comprehend much better when they employ the reading strategies outlined in this book. Almost all of my students volunteer to participate in my class after their first instructional session because they see that with just some adjustment in their approach they can understand what they are reading.

The vast majority of children whom I have taught using these instructional strategies on a consistent basis have experienced significant improvement in reading comprehension as evidenced by their own and their families' opinions, as well as their grades on tests and on their report cards.

chapter 2

What Kids Most Want to Know

The Cloze Reading Strategy

Fourth-grader Joy's retelling of material from a book she has silently read shows that she understands far less than I expected she would since the English is not too complex for her and she is familiar with the subject matter. I wonder why she doesn't understand more of what she is reading.

I invite Joy to "read" the same text orally—letting her say the words out loud. Most of the time she says real words or made-up words that begin with letters similar to those of the unfamiliar words but which make no sense in context, such as *gorning* for *grieving*. When I ask what she thinks *gorning* might mean, she has no idea or no idea that makes sense in context. This behavior indicates that she would probably benefit from Cloze Reading Strategy lessons that would show her how to look to the context for hints about the author's meaning. When Joy begins to use these strategies automatically, she will understand the gist of many more sentences containing unfamiliar words.

When to Teach the Cloze Reading Strategy

Like Joy, most developing readers' first concern is all the words they do not know. These developing readers believe that they are not reading well unless they name every single word correctly. Their full attention is on naming words, and they cannot pay attention to anything else. This is understandable, since one cannot read without recognizing words, and children are taught many useful strategies for learning new words in school. However, this natural desire to know more words can become an obstacle to comprehension when a developing reader obsessively insists on naming *all* words, including those which, in themselves, will mean nothing at all to her, even should she succeed in pronouncing them correctly. Better readers have a different strategy. When they are confronted with unfamiliar words that they have no hope of pronouncing, they try to understand the surrounding context. Cloze Reading Strategy lessons address this reflex response of stopping until every single word is named, and remove this obstruction to reading better by making reading less a process of precise word identification and more a process of constructing meaning.

How to Teach the Cloze Reading Strategy

The Cloze Reading Strategy answers the question "How do I deal with unfamiliar words?" Students are invited to create working definitions of unfamiliar words in context. This strategy is used by all proficient readers when there is enough contextual information to enable them to form a hypothesis—but most proficient readers are not conscious of what they are naturally doing.

The first thing that students want to know is what to do about words they don't know and can't pronounce. The Cloze Reading Strategy lesson imitates the reading situation in which students face several unfamiliar words in a section with enough familiar context to enable plausible guessing about what they may mean. The proficient reader will automatically read through the context, seeking clues to create working definitions for the unfamiliar words—provided there is enough familiar meaning surrounding the unknown words.

The cloze exercises often found in language arts workbooks can *look* like a Cloze Reading Strategy lesson. Both can be a single paragraph with several blanks to be filled in. The difference is that in a Cloze Reading Strategy lesson the reader is expected to generate the meanings that will "close up" the paragraph so that it makes sense. In this practice, just as in students' actual reading experiences, the reader is never given a list of words or phrases to choose from to put into the slots. The students learn to think like good readers, and that includes creating working definitions for unfamiliar words without the support of a list of suggestions; instead, they get practice generating choices through a process that more closely resembles their experience in reading.

Paired-Paragraph Cloze Strategy Lessons

The paired-paragraph lessons that follow are substantially different from typical cloze exercises in that they require the learner to read through the context before deciding what might go into the blanks and make sense. Taken in pairs, the nearly identical cloze paragraphs, differing only in their endings, make the point to the developing reader that it is usually necessary to search throughout the context to find enough clues to decide what the unfamiliar words might mean.

Procedure

Example #1 is paired with Example #2. In each case, show the reader the sentences gradually until the entire story is revealed. Keep the last sentence hidden, then reveal it after all the guessing has simmered down.

Example 1

I am not happy. My _____ is broken. Now I can't _____ because it won't _____. My mother said someone will come to fix it tomorrow. I hope so. I like to _____ when I get home. I am a big baseball and basketball fan! I love to watch the Yankees and the Nets when they are playing.

Example 2

I am not happy. My _____ is broken. Now I can't _____ because it won't _____. My mother said someone will come to fix it tomorrow. I hope so. I like to _____ it when I get home. I like to peddle around the park.

See Appendixes on page 88 for reproducible versions of these exercises and those that follow. (Reproducible 2.1)

Aliens in the House Cloze Strategy Lessons

Another form of the Cloze Reading Strategy lesson is to present words alien to most students, but to present them in familiar contexts.

Procedure

Invite students to make logical predictions of the meaning of the sentences as well as the unknown words. An example of the use of unfamiliar words in familiar contexts is the classroom rules I use during the first instructional day.

Classroom Rules

How to Behave in Ms. Lazar's Room

- Do not speak when someone else is expounding.

- Elevate your hand and wait to be called on.

- Do not frolic with other students in class.
  You can do that on the playground.

After the students have generated at least two plausible meanings for each unfamiliar word, they look up their meanings in the thesaurus. The best book for making this point is *The Clear and Simple Thesaurus Dictionary* by Wittles, Greisman, and Morris (1996). Its layout makes it perfectly clear to students what the target words are and what their synonyms are. (Kids love this book, by the way, because its layout makes it easy to catch on to the meaning of a word.) When students see how accurate their predictions are, they gain confidence in themselves and immediately become less afraid of written language.

What a Word Means Doesn't Necessarily Look Like the Word Itself

I take this opportunity to point out that what a word means usually looks nothing like the word itself looks. For example, *elevate* means *lift* or *raise*; *frolic* means *play*. Because believing that words' meanings begin with the same sounds as the words themselves is such a common mistake among many developing readers, I spend the next half hour checking lists and lists of words. When I teach a small group of third graders, I invite each student to randomly pick any page in the thesaurus. Then, they close their eyes and pick any word. I ask them to check to see whether the word's synonym looks similar to the word. The kids are stunned to find that most of the time the synonym looks nothing like the word. So I try again. Another student, another page, another word, same result. Now this is getting weird—and challenging to their expectations. The children want to be sure. So I look down any page in the thesaurus with the same result. Perhaps one or two words out of the 20 words listed on the page look like their synonyms. "So what does that suggest?" I ask.

The students come to realize that it means you can think of *any* synonym that works in context. Most of the time, the synonym will not look anything at all like the word. Next, I take a closer look at the list of synonyms and notice something else that is just as liberating. Sometimes a word's "synonym" is not just one word; it is, instead, an entire phrase. "So what does that suggest?" I probe. Readers do not have to think of just one word to substitute for the unknown word! "Eureka! Freedom at last!" Students can substitute an entire phrase for an unknown word as long as it makes sense in context.

Now readers know that when sounding out is not working for them, they have the intellectual freedom and right to think of any logical meaning for an unfamiliar word—irrespective of how it looks or sounds. This gives developing readers such a feeling of freedom and hope. *Now print does not have to control them—now they can control print! Now they get it!*

Begin With Oral Work

To get the most from Cloze Reading Strategy lessons, it is best to begin with oral work. I have also found that using consistent language to present and reiterate the cloze process helps students more readily remember the steps involved.

Whenever I read anything, I try to understand what it is about. **Goal of Reading**

To help the children gain a deep understanding of a particular reading strategy, I have them work hard to memorize brief statements or coaching questions about the strategy. I call these statements "mantras." The first mantra I teach is "The Goal of Reading," which is this: "Whenever I read anything, I try to understand what it is about."

Students must be able to say their reading goal whenever I ask them, no matter what they are doing—skipping, standing in line, eating snacks, whatever—so it becomes fun for them. They often beg me to ask them at the most ludicrous times.

The next mantra I have the children work hard to memorize is the main coaching question that they will ask themselves for the rest of their lives whenever they do not understand what they are reading: "What could this mean that would make sense to me? Make three predictions!"

The children can recite this at a drop of a hat, and even remember it in later grades. My students tell me that these "sayings" really help them understand more when the reading gets tough. All mantras are included as in the appendix on page 127.

> Ask yourself, "What could this mean that would make sense to me?" Then tell yourself, "Make three predictions!"

One-Sentence Cloze Lessons

Start by helping students understand the concept of "what would make sense." Give them this example orally:

I love chocolate mworu *in my milk.*

Ask them for the meaning of *mworu*. "Would *mice* make sense? Would *money* make sense? Would *elephant* make sense?" Notice that the first two predictions were based only on the initial letter of the mystery word *mworu*. Many students will, at first, guess words that begin with the same sound as the mystery word. The third prediction is something silly designed to make the students laugh. They are laughing because they know that *elephant* just does not make sense—and that is your teaching point: to have them begin to understand the difference between making sense and not making sense.

Show more oral examples in which students can predict a single word or phrase (a group of words) to make a sentence complete. For example,

I am very late for eoweo, *and my coach will be angry.*

Students are likely to fill in the *eoweo* blank with such predictions as *baseball practice*, *swimming practice*, or *the soccer game*—here two or three words supply the possible meaning of *eoweo* and complete the sentence in a logical way. In order to know which meaning is correct, readers would have to inquire of the speaker in order to get more clues or confirmation as to which logically possible answer is correct and which logically possible answers are not. Many possible answers—such as *Mars*, or *church*, or *my birthday*—will have been eliminated by the students on the basis of their not being logical completers of the sentence.

Proceed to Written Work

Once students begin to grasp the meaning of "what would make sense?" you are ready to begin written-language Cloze Reading Strategy lessons. Start with simple one-sentence examples of very familiar topics and language.

I raise my appendage when I want my teacher to call on me.

Students should be told to "hum" over the unknown word or words, and get to the end of the sentence. Have students point to the periods at the ends of the sentences before they actually read the text. Just let them find the periods. Tell them that when they come to a word they don't know, "just hum over it and keep reading until you get to the period." They should try to picture in their minds the meaning of the sentence. Next, they must make three predictions as to the logically possible meaning of the word. They must then test their predictions for logic in the context of the sentence, and say "good-bye" to predictions that no longer make sense.

Remind students that they can predict a single word or a group of words to make the sentence complete. It is important to teach them to pay attention to the function words (i.e., articles, prepositions, demonstrative pronouns, conjunctions) in the sentences because they help the reader a lot in figuring out what might make sense.

Two-Sentence Cloze Lessons (More Aliens in the House)

Here's an easy way to get started.

Procedure

Go on to simple, two-sentence written examples with very familiar topics and language, such as this:

My father is concocting tonight's meal. I hope it tastes good.

Point out that sometimes you have to read past the period and go on to the next sentence to get a hint about what the writing could be about.

Next, present longer sentences with familiar topics and language such as:

I looked ludicrous in my brand-new suit. I was supposed to wear it at my graduation, but I felt foolish.

Ask students for three predictions of the possible logical meaning of the unfamiliar word.

Demonstrate that a reader could predict opposites, if both made sense. Opposite meanings could cover two of the requisite three predictions. For example, *ludicrous* might mean "handsome," "homely," or "smokin'." With the students, say "good-bye" to any predictions that do not make sense.

Present even longer complex sentences.

I look dapper in my brand-new suit, which I am thrilled to wear to my graduation next week.

Have the students "hum" over the unknown word and try to picture the meaning of the longer sentence in their minds. Apply the same process of making three predictions and evaluating whether they are logically possible with the students.

Multi-Sentence Cloze Lessons

In all of the above Cloze Reading Strategy lessons, please feel free to add a sentence that hints at one or another of the students' predictions. This makes the all-important point that, most times, the reader needs more information than is contained in a single sentence to figure out the meaning of unfamiliar words and phrases.

For example, the text says: *There was ample candy in the bag for everyone.*

The class predicts the following meanings for *ample*: "a lot of," "no," "sweet," "chocolate," "plenty of."

To illustrate that more information is necessary, you might ask: "If the next sentence were *Everyone got two pieces,* what might *ample* mean? To which choices would I have to say 'good-bye'?"

You could then ask, again: "If the next sentence were *No one got any candy,* what might *ample* mean? To which choices would I have to say 'good-bye'?"

Finally, ask: "If the next sentence were *The candy melted all over our fingers,* what might *ample* mean?"

Create Your Own Cloze Reading Strategy Lessons

The beauty of these lessons is that they are so easy to create! The level of their difficulty is easily controlled and they can be used with a single reader or with a group of readers working together. It's fun to see how the addition of information changes what is logically possible and likely to be a correct answer. This also demonstrates how important the context of the rest of the text is in helping a reader to understand more precisely what the writer intended.

Making Cloze Reading Strategy Lessons From Fictional Works

Cloze Reading Strategy lessons can be made from the texts that students are reading or from texts they might be interested in reading. Let's start with fiction. Select an easy passage from a picture book or another simple book appropriate in difficulty for your students. Make sure that there are enough useful context clues upon which students can base their predictions. Copy the page onto an overhead transparency (or display on a Smart Board). Have student volunteers walk up to the page and cross out the word(s) they do not recognize. What remains of the text are the words that almost everyone in the class knows. The students should read the altered text and, in pairs, decide what the sentences probably mean, filling in the blanks so that the entire class has closure and makes sense of the passage.

Since some words are familiar to one student but completely alien to another, and students who recognize the *alien* words would love to call them out, I ask my students to follow the Word-Telling Rule (see opposite page). All the students cooperate because they understand that this rule allows each of them the time and quiet to think about the meaning of the puzzling words and phrases.

Start with something very simple and funny. For beginning readers, something with two or three sentences on a page and pictures illustrating the story works well. For more advanced readers, you'll use texts with more words and fewer pictures—but still put just one page on an overhead transparency. Eventually, when you think the students are ready, show a page of fiction that is purely text, with no pictures. At this point, students must rely exclusively upon the written language, their own efforts, and logic to comprehend the text.

Making Cloze Reading Strategy Lessons From Nonfiction Texts

Graduate to informational text. Follow the same process, gradually increasing the difficulty, age-appropriately, with informational text. Informational text can be trickier because sometimes the unfamiliar word is also an unfamiliar idea to the reader, so the initial one-page nonfiction pieces should be about topics that are extremely familiar to students. Depending upon the ability and experience of your students, start with an appropriately simple text containing one to three sentences supported by photographs or illustrations. Then, in stages, present one page with more text and fewer photographs until you show only text unsupported by illustrations of any kind. Here, too, the students must rely exclusively upon their own use of logic and written language to comprehend.

Word-Telling Rule

Unless I give you permission to do otherwise, here is the rule:

Do not say words out loud.

1. Do not say a word out loud unless the teacher asks you to do so.

2. Do not tell a student a word, even if he or she asks.

3. Do not read a word out loud, so others can hear.

4. Do not whisper a word out loud.

5. Do not try to help a student by telling him or her a word (unless you are working in a group).

6. DO NOT SHOW OFF by saying a word out loud.

Teaching Points

As developing readers try to apply the Cloze Reading Strategy with real text, they will run into situations that mature readers know how to deal with, but developing readers do not. Make sure your developing readers learn the following simple rules about reading. In general, you will find that the more your students know about, pay attention to, and are fascinated by language, the more relentless and the more successful they will be in their search for the author's meaning in the texts they read.

Read Past the Word

The student should first tell himself what the sentence is probably about. If he is not sure, he should redo the same procedure, close his eyes, and try to picture the meaning of the sentence. Sometimes it helps if pairs of students are doing this together. One person says the sentence and "hums" over the unknown word, and the other tries to paraphrase its meaning.

Try to Read the Function Words Correctly

You will want to make this *crucial* point to the students: it is the function words (articles, prepositions, demonstrative pronouns, and conjunctions)—often "little words"—that are important, sometimes more important than the "big words" (nouns, verbs, personal and relative pronouns, adverbs, and adjectives), in helping you to understand what is going on. Function words help connect and show the relationship between other words in the sentence. Once students begin to read past the unknown word, they begin to notice the little words before and after "the word" that provide so much information about what the sentence is probably about. Students should try to be exact when reading such little words as *in, on, with, for, to, and, into, the,* and *this,* to name just a few. These function words provide the strongest hints about what the sentence and the unfamiliar word could mean. Kids may not believe this at first. But the more students use the little words successfully to infer sentences' meanings, the more they will pay attention to them before and after the unknown word.

Make Three Sensible Predictions for Every Unknown Word or Phrase

Do not allow students to stop after saying the first thing that pops into their heads—whether it makes sense or not. You want them to really think about the possibilities so that they can understand the author irrespective of the direction he may take in the writing. When students make three predictions, often the first prediction makes almost no sense because the student is relying on the letters of the word instead of its possible meaning. Often the second makes some sense, but not the best sense. It is usually the student's third or fourth prediction that comes close to sensible meaning, and it often is a synonym for the unknown word. *Please do not lead students to the "right" answer.* These lessons work only when the student has earned his understanding by applying effort and logic.

Predict an Idea and Its Opposite

If both the idea and its opposite could make sense in context, then make a third likely prediction. The proficient reader realizes that both are possible at this point in the text. She will decide to read on, hunting carefully for clues that point to the idea or its opposite, or to something else entirely. For example, if a proficient reader reads the sentence *The movie was stupendous* and does not recognize the word *stupendous,* she might think that two predictions are equally likely—the movie was "bad" or the move was "good." She would be alert for clues in context that hint at either of these predictions or another one that she did not think of, such as *frightening* or *boring.*

Recognize That Many Words Mean *Said*

Have students learn the conventions of print, such as commas and quotation marks, that tell alert readers that a word probably means *said.*

Call Proper Nouns by Their First Letters

After taking the pressure off, by following this rule students should try to figure out what these words represent in the text. (More about this appears in Chapter 3, which focuses on the Nicknaming Reading Strategy.)

Use Endings Added to Words to Help You Understand the Words

When students become relaxed about employing the Cloze Reading Strategy, then start to draw their attention to the endings added to the root words by adding them to the "hum." Examples would be: *hummed, humming, humly, hums, hummer, hummier, hummiest.* This helps the reader understand the sentence better, if he had not been paying attention to the bound morphemes. When you see the light in your students' eyes indicating that they get this little trick, you can go on to their next big worry—pronouncing the proper names of people, places, and things.

Frequently Asked Questions

I. Is it really so important for students to have practice generating three or more possible meanings for unfamiliar words?

Absolutely! It is critical for developing readers to know that they have the intellectual capacity to come up with more than one possible prediction. Ineffective readers may come up with one prediction, but if that idea does not really help them understand, they stop trying. Better readers are not so easily discouraged. They know from experience that they are capable of thinking of many likely meanings for the unknown word. They are confident because they are ready to go in almost any direction the author may choose to take them.

On the other hand, of course, sometimes the meaning of a sentence is so obvious that only one prediction could fit. But your goal is to give your students the exhilarating experience of thinking logically about the many things an author might mean.

2. Are Cloze Reading Strategy lessons a suggestion that students should not look up the meanings of unfamiliar words?

No. Cloze Reading Strategy lessons constitute an additional tool for you to use with your students, rather than a replacement for the all-important work of learning the definitions of words. The Cloze Reading Strategy merely highlights for students how useful context can be when there are no dictionaries, thesauruses, computers, or people around to help explain the meanings of unfamiliar words.

3. How long does it take for students to begin to use this strategy automatically?

The speed of learning to apply the Cloze Reading Strategy automatically depends on the usual factors:

♦ How many opportunities students have had to practice the strategy with teacher-made lessons

♦ How many opportunities the students have had to apply the strategy with authentic text, including sharing and discussing inferences and rationales with peers

♦ How logically students can think in general—if a student has trouble reasoning, then the progress is slower

4. Does learning the Cloze Reading Strategy really improve students' reading comprehension?

Yes. The improvement is enormous. Most learners improve their comprehension to a very significant degree. After all, the students have given up their ineffective strategies aimed at merely pronouncing words and have decided instead to try to understand the author. You see the change not only in the amount and quality of the students' comprehension, but in their demeanor: they are more hopeful and more confident. And, in general, they are more attentive in class.

Mr. Mxyzptlk, or What Do I Do If I Can't Pronounce This Name?

The Nicknaming Reading Strategy

Annie makes long pauses at unfamiliar proper nouns. Like all of us, she does not know how to pronounce some of the names she encounters in fiction or in informational text. What is unusual is that she spends an inordinate amount of time trying to pronounce these names correctly. After finally deciding upon a name (or just skipping over the name), Annie may have little or no idea what that name represents in the text.

When to Teach the Nicknaming Reading Strategy

If Annie or one of your students exhibits this pattern, with fiction especially, then she would probably benefit from Nicknaming Reading Strategy lessons. These lessons teach her to do two things: to name the proper noun by using its initial letter and to search the context for hints and clues about the function of that person, place, or thing in the text.

How to Teach the Nicknaming Reading Strategy

The Nicknaming Reading Strategy invites learners to name each unfamiliar proper noun by its first letter, and then to figure out its function in the text. Good readers employ this strategy whenever they are confronted by unfamiliar proper nouns.

The Nicknaming Reading Strategy lesson replicates the reading situation of being confronted with a lot of unfamiliar proper nouns. The proficient reader may call the name by its first letter while searching the context for clues as to its function. Developing readers find that the nicknaming lesson is a very useful reminder of how to focus on the meaning of the text instead of becoming frightened and overwhelmed by a plethora of unfamiliar names of people, places, or things.

The following Nicknaming Reading Strategy lesson requires that the reader be precise about the function of each proper noun. The tricky part in this story is that there are *two* "owners." One is the owner of the dog, and one is the owner of the bakery. The lesson makes the point that when assigning a function to a proper noun, the reader must be precise. Students find the story below funny and challenging. See page 96 for the reproducible.

Example 1

Histmanitnlaoria and the Bistominstao Sweet Shoppe

By Simiotminoanintianotnekondoanei Reinsod

Histmanitnlaoria was a little, gray, furry dog. He was lost and could not find his way home. He was looking in town for his owner.

Histmanitnlaoria passed by the bakery called The Bistominstao Sweet Shoppe. Ms. Bistominstao saw the dog and came outside. She said, "Hi, Histmanitnlaoria! I am glad to see you. Your owner, Mr. Rishtonema, is looking for you. Stay here and eat a cookie."

Ms. Bistominstao kept Histmanitnlaoria in The Bistominstao's Sweet Shoppe until Mr. Rishtonema showed up. Mr. Rishtonema was so happy to have Histmanitnlaoria back!

Procedure

Have students follow the steps below to engage with the story and involve them in conversation about it.

- Read the story silently. Turn the page over and write one sentence explaining what the story might be about.

- Now circle the first letter of every name in the title and the first letter of the author's first and last names.

- Do the same thing in the story. Circle the first letter of every name in the story. Hint: You should find that you have circled several *H*s, *R*s, and *B*s.

- Read the story saying only the first letter of each name instead of trying to pronounce the characters' actual names.

- Turn the page over and write one sentence explaining what you now think the story might be about.

- Which way was easier for you to understand the story: trying to pronounce each and every name, or just calling each name by its first letter? Why?

- Complete these sentences and underline the clues in the story you used to figure this out.

H probably is _____.

The B Sweet Shoppe probably is

_____.

Ms. B probably is _____.

Mr. R probably is _____.

Objectives of Nicknaming Reading Strategy Lessons

Students should end up having several insights about dealing with unfamiliar proper nouns as a result of these lessons. They include the following:

- No matter how many unpronounceable proper nouns the text has, the reader can understand the author to some degree.

- The reader's responsibility is to assign a function to each proper noun even though the reader may not be able to pronounce its name.

- The reader does not have to pronounce the proper noun correctly; he just has to give it a nickname, and then stick with that same made-up nick name throughout the piece.

- It is easiest and wisest to use the initial letter of a proper noun as its nickname.

- If two proper nouns start with the same letter(s), then use the first few letters for their nicknames.

- The reader's main effort should be to hunt actively for information about the function of each proper noun throughout the text.

- Proper nouns always start with a capital letter, and each proper noun stands for a particular name of a person, place, or thing.

- Sentences always begin with capital letters, so the reader has to decide which words are actually proper nouns and which are not.

- Once the reader has decided what the role of each proper noun is in the text, the reader should use that role as a "name" for the proper noun. This helps the reader have a higher level of comprehension.

- In fiction, it does not matter what the proper noun is called as long as the name is appropriate to the gender and species. Most of the time, the nickname does not change the story.

- In nonfiction, it does matter what you call the proper noun after having read the text all the way through. Sometimes the nickname is only temporary until the reader has enough information to know from prior knowledge the factual name of that person, place, or thing. The reader might progress from "W," to a place beginning with "W," to a city beginning with "W," to "Washington, D.C."

Making Nicknaming Reading Strategy Lessons

It is best to use very long, even daunting, unpronounceable names when creating Nicknaming Reading Strategy lessons. This is intended to discourage the reader from spending a lot of time trying to say the name. Some readers may make the efficient decision to merely nickname the long proper noun and get on with trying to understand the text. Other readers may decide to do what they have always done—work at naming the beast. Naming the beast, at this point, will not get the reader any closer to understanding the text, so this reading decision proves to be a waste of time, effort, and intellect. Through repeated practice with the Nicknaming Reading Strategy, the reader will find that when she decides to stop trying to name the proper noun correctly, she will be able to understand more of the meaning of the text.

Possible Topics for Nicknaming Reading Strategy Lessons

♦ Everyday events that happen to children and families (narrative)

♦ Imitations of informational texts being read by the students, or that the students would like to read

Increasing the Level of Difficulty of Nicknaming Reading Strategy Lessons

♦ Easier—Use three or four sentences with only one or two proper nouns to deal with

♦ Harder—Include more sentences, more unfamiliar proper nouns, and more subtle information that the readers must use to infer the function of each proper noun

Telling Doesn't Work

Nicknaming proper nouns is not a new concept to many teachers; however, simply advising students to create nicknames for these nouns, without the experience of the search for meaning that is prompted by the Nicknaming Reading Strategy lessons, generally produces less satisfying results. Here are three things that you may have found yourself saying to your students, with an explanation of how they are similar to but different from teaching Nicknaming Reading Strategy lessons.

♦ *Just give it a nickname and keep reading!* Teachers often tell children to do this, but this alone does not seem to help kids deal with proper names effectively. This is because *telling* does not work well. Nicknaming Reading Strategy lessons put children through the thinking process that all effective readers employ automatically when confronted with unfamiliar proper nouns. The more times the learners experience these kinds of lessons, the more they will understand what to do and why. After a series of Nicknaming Reading Strategy lessons of increasing difficulty, the teacher will never again have to *tell* the strategy. It is far better to let the children experience the strategy through guided reading strategy lessons.

♦ *Make up any name.* Teachers sometimes give students this advice. But it is not the best idea. Children quickly forget the names they make up, and so lose track of the proper noun and its function. The information that surrounds the name is lost, because the reader keeps making up different names for the same proper noun. Also, children sometimes make up a name that affects the meaning of the story in a way unintended by the author. For example, at the start of a story, students sometimes assign a girl's name to a male character or vice versa. If they keep the incorrectly gendered name throughout the story, it is a strong indication that these children are not trying to understand the text but instead are just trying to get through it. When children use the first letter of the unknown proper noun, they will not forget the nickname, and they will not lose information attached to each proper noun.

♦ *Don't worry about the name—just figure out what the name stands for in the text.* Again, teachers often tell children *to do* this, but it does not seem to happen. Most kids don't do it. Instead they stay focused on the unfamiliar name and keep trying to pronounce it. Why don't the kids do what the teacher is telling them to do? Because *telling* does not work as well as Nicknaming Reading Strategy lessons do. A mark of a proficient reader is one who will be able to determine the function of unpronounceable proper nouns from contextual clues. This is not an easy skill to acquire; however, it is one that readers can be taught through the use of gradually more complex Nicknaming Reading Strategy lessons.

"Tell Yourself Each Name's Function Each Time You See That Name in the Text"

One of the really important insights that readers gain from Nicknaming Reading Strategy lessons is to look for clues about the function of each proper noun. Once the function has been determined, the reader should tell himself that function every time he comes across that particular proper noun. This little trick helps readers maintain a very high level of understanding while reading.

In the previous story about the Sweet Shoppe on page 31, for example, my students read the entire last paragraph:

> *"Ms. Bistominstao kept Histmanitnlaoria in The Bistominstao's Sweet Shoppe until Mr. Rishtonema showed up. Mr. Rishtonema was so happy to have Histmanitnlaoria back!"*

as follows, to help them to understand the story with crystal clarity:

> *"The bakery owner kept the dog in the bakery until the owner of the dog showed up. The owner of the dog was so happy to have the dog back."*

Substituting the meaning of each proper noun for the noun itself helps to clarify the meaning for the student and confirms the students' understanding for the teacher.

Teaching Points

The Nicknaming Reading Strategy lessons teach children tricks that accomplished readers already know about the most effective ways to understand the author, even when the proper nouns are unfamiliar.

♦ Invite students to read the Nicknaming Reading Strategy lesson without help.

♦ Instruct students to write on the back of the page what they think the piece is about.

♦ Talk about what made the piece hard to understand. The answer is almost always the unfamiliar proper nouns.

♦ Remind students that their goal is to try to understand whatever they read.

♦ Ask learners to suggest ways of dealing with unfamiliar names, since they occur frequently when children read. Some will say they would sound the name out. Discuss how well that strategy works with new and difficult proper nouns. Has it helped them to understand the text or not? Elicit other ideas about dealing with unfamiliar names. Often, someone in the class has already figured out and is using this strategy and will talk about nicknaming, although he may not call it that.

♦ Ask whether students want to know how excellent readers deal with unfamiliar names.

♦ Sometimes it is a good idea to use a newspaper at this point. The first page is generally filled with unfamiliar names from such countries as Sudan, Iraq, Iran, and Pakistan. Demonstrate nicknaming with the newspaper, and what the proper nouns probably represent in the text (e.g., name of a place in Pakistan, name of an important person in Iraq). Go back to the newspaper after the Nicknaming Reading Strategy lesson has been completed so the children can see again how an excellent reader applies this strategy to real situations.

Frequently Asked Questions

1. **Do you ever teach children that it is important to pronounce a name correctly?**

    Yes. Proficient readers have specific purposes for reading something. If they want more information about, say, President Barack Obama, it will be important for them to be able to recognize that name in writing. The children should never be discouraged from trying to name precisely the real people, places, and things that they must know for school. But if they cannot pronounce a proper name, they cannot just give up. They still have to gather information about that name until they realize to what or to whom the proper noun is referring, or until someone tells them how to pronounce it.

2. **Is that what you tell the students—that, usually, you learn to pronounce the names of real people, places, and things by having someone who knows tell you?**

    Yes. That is how most of us learn to pronounce names correctly—someone has told us. One can guess at the pronunciation but will not know for sure until he hears someone who knows the correct pronunciation say it.

chapter 4

The Most Powerful Tool I Know

The Scattered Clues Reading Strategy

Despite my best efforts with Cloze Reading Strategy lessons, Jack continues to make only one prediction when confronted with unfamiliar words or phrases in material that he understands well when it's read to him. That one prediction usually does not come close to the author's intended meaning. When he cannot come up with a sensible guess on his first try, Jack just gives up. He thinks that if he has not figured out a workable meaning with his first guess, then he is incapable of doing it.

Jack has another obstacle to improved reading comprehension. He does not change his predictions about what the author might mean even when confronted with information that challenges his ideas. He seems to ignore important information that points to an entirely different meaning than what he thinks is the point of the text. Jack is still not really responding to the context. Instead he is merely saying words in his head.

Why Teach the Scattered Clues Reading Strategy

Scattered Clues Reading Strategy lessons will put Jack through the process of thinking of more than one possible meaning for each bit of unfamiliar text. He will be amazed at himself when he realizes that if he just pushes himself to think of more than one possibility, he will come close to the author's meaning most of the time. Scattered Clues Reading Strategy lessons will show Jack how to incorporate information gathered throughout the text in order to come to an understanding closer to the author's intention. Jack's approach to understanding print will change considerably. Instead of ignoring clues, he will seek them out. Instead of having just one idea about what the author might mean, Jack will have several.

The "Goal of Reading" should be displayed and memorized by students like a mantra before starting this series of practice lessons:

Goal of Reading

Whenever I read anything, I try to understand what it is about.

What Is a Clue?

- A clue is a bit of information that you search for and locate.

- A clue is a bit of information that you understand and can say in your own words.

- A clue is a bit of information that you use to help you to understand the author.

- A clue is a bit of information that you use to infer and predict the author's possible meaning as you create a working hypothesis.

How to Teach the Scattered Clues Reading Strategy

The Scattered Clues Reading Strategy is powerful because it imitates the reading process precisely. Students learn that reading is a logical predicting process and that the reader must often force himself to generate several possible predictions and then change those predictions when they are evaluated against the criteria of new information gained by reading further through the text. Ideally, the reader is ultimately able to infer a working hypothesis as to the author's probable meaning.

Predict—to foretell on the basis of observation, experience, or scientific reason

Infer—to arrive at a conclusion by reasoning from evidence

Hypothesize—to make a tentative assumption in order to draw out and test its logical or empirical consequences

The Scattered Clues Reading Strategy is the single most powerful reading strategy that I have used with learners of any age. As the name suggests, lessons for this strategy imitate real reading situations when the author's clues are scattered throughout the text, and it is the reader's job to actively search for these clues and use them logically in order to try to infer the meaning of any part of the writing. Scattered Clues Reading Strategy lessons highlight for learners that comprehension is a logical predicting and confirming process and put them through the mental activity of generating a series of plausible predictions when confronted with clues from the author that appear throughout the text.

Scattered Clues Reading Strategy Lesson #1

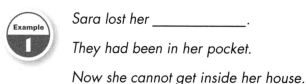

Example 1

Sara lost her _____.

They had been in her pocket.

Now she cannot get inside her house.

Scattered Clues Reading Strategy Lesson #1 serves to highlight the author's use of pronouns such as they. Pronouns are often ignored by developing readers who consequently understand less than they otherwise might.

It is very important that students are shown one sentence at a time and are invited to make predictions about the possible meaning of each sentence. Please note that either a word, or a whole phrase, can fill the blank left for the missing language. The goal is to have the first sentence make sense with a variety of predictions. Once that is done, the second sentence is revealed to the students. When only two sentences are showing, the learners must "say good-bye" to all predictions that no longer make sense, eliminating nonsensical predictions.

They must also refine all existing predictions that might still make sense. And the students must add new predictions based upon the newly revealed clue. The final sentence points to one likely inference, which students are asked to articulate. They are also asked to generate a backup hypothesis, in the way that proficient readers often do.

Scattered Clues Reading Strategy
Lesson #2

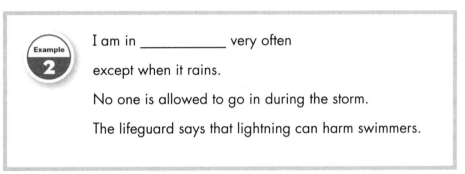

Example 2

I am in _____ very often

except when it rains.

No one is allowed to go in during the storm.

The lifeguard says that lightning can harm swimmers.

Lesson #2 serves to highlight both the Scattered Clues Reading Strategy and the author's use of negatives such as *except*. Negative and conditional phrases (e.g., *no, not, never, except, until*) are often ignored by developing readers who end up with a completely different understanding than the author intended. When more than one logically feasible possibility is mentioned by students, this is your opportunity to say that authors do not always provide conclusive information. And sometimes, the best that a good reader can do is to hold in her head several likely possibilities and hope that the author eventually points more directly to one particular choice.

Use the "Make Three Predictions" Mantra to Help Students

Begin the discussion of each scattered clues exercise with this invitation: "Ask yourself, 'What could this mean that would make sense to me?' Then tell yourself, 'Make three predictions!'" These are not random predictions. They are reasoned hypotheses based upon the context, the reader's prior knowledge, and the reader's use of logic. Usually the first prediction is off the mark and based on only a portion of the context— the most obvious part of the context. When the reader evaluates that idea against more of the context, she realizes she must find a better answer. So she tries to think of another possibility. This second hypothesis is generally better because it reflects consideration of more of the text, and the reader has used more logical thinking. Many children want to quit after the second guess. They figure they came close to something that makes sense. They fear that it might be

> Ask yourself, "What could this mean that would make sense to me?" Then tell yourself, "Make three predictions!"

too hard, too much work, and probably hopeless anyway for them to try to come up with an even better idea. But if you insist, by quietly waiting for the student to think it through with more effort and more thought, the student usually comes up with a really good idea that makes a lot of sense within the entire context. The child stuns herself nine times out of ten. Her eyes get big and she knows deep inside her that she has thought of a great idea. Her hand shoots up, and she waves it madly, hardly able to contain herself. If the teacher asks at this point whether she thinks she has something that really makes sense, the child grins hugely and nods enthusiastically. She is certain she has figured it out. It is a great moment because *no one* led her to this answer. *No one* gave any hints. *No one* helped in any way other than to teach her to think logically of three predictions that might make sense within the entire context. And when this student keeps doing this—keeps surprising herself by thinking of logical and plausible ideas—she begins to sit up straight and feel confident that she can understand what she reads and, even better, that she, indeed, has the intelligence to master reading instead of feeling that walls of words will always and forever have mastery over her.

It is very important to keep pointing out to your students after they have thought carefully, worked hard, and figured something out that they did this by themselves. This is the point at which students decide to learn to read better, because they believe they can.

Sample Dialogue Between Teacher and Student

"Did anyone help you?"

"No."

"Did I give you any hints?"

"No."

"Did you do this all by yourself?"

"Yes."

"Are you surprised at yourself?"

"YES!"

"When you are at home and reading to yourself, will you keep doing this trick of really thinking about the writing and asking yourself, 'What could this mean that would make sense to me?' And then also make three predictions?"

"Yes, yes, yes!"

And many children do continue to use this strategy. They think they have been shown a very special trick that will work, and they are glad. Their teachers are often very surprised by the change in comprehension the child is showing after having experienced only a few Scattered Clues Reading Strategy lessons.

How to Construct Scattered Clues Reading Strategy Lessons

In writing Scattered Clues Reading Strategy lessons for beginners, you will want to keep these guidelines in mind.

♦ Keep the students guessing actively until the very last clue is revealed. It is essential that the meaning of the first sentence remains ambiguous until the final clue is revealed, since when we read authentic material, the author's meaning is often ambiguous to us, and the best we can do to infer the author's meaning is consider all the clues and decide as logically as we can what the author might mean.

♦ Have each clue generate a few new predictions, eliminate a few past predictions, and, if possible, refine some past predictions, too.

♦ The blank should take the place of either a word or a phrase that is very familiar to the students.

♦ Possible topics for Scattered Clues Reading Strategy lessons:

  • Everyday occurrences

  • Facts that kids don't know but would find funny or surprising (a good source is *National Geographic Kids* Magazine)

  • Popular subject matter from children's magazines and Web sites

  • Retold regional stories (urban, farm, from the local press or news)

Increasing the Level of Difficulty of Scattered Clues Reading Strategy Lessons

All Scattered Clues Reading Strategy lessons contain very familiar topics with very common language. The level of difficulty of the lessons increases starting from the easiest, which have three simple sentences, to the more difficult, which have four longer, complex sentences.

Easy—The first sentence contains a blank. The second sentence provides a clue to the meaning of the blank in the first sentence. The third sentence gives enough information to enable the reader to decide how to fill in the blank.

Moderate—At the next level, the lesson contains four simple sentences. Although structured in a similar way, at this level, the third sentence makes the learner think about an entirely different idea than she had been aiming at.

Difficult—For more difficult lessons, again choose a very familiar topic, with very common language, but use four longer sentences. The longer sentences should highlight a particular aspect of written language such as negatives, pronouns, referents, or embedded clauses. You can customize the lessons to the particular challenges your students are experiencing in their current reading in your class or in other classes they are taking. The most difficult lessons will contain many embedded clauses, some unfamiliar words and proper nouns, but in order to be successful, the lesson must contain enough information to enable learners to infer a probable meaning of the missing word or phrase.

I have found that it is essential to make the connection immediately and clearly between the Scattered Clues Reading Strategy lesson and learning to read better throughout the entire procedure. The children enjoy this lesson so much that they sometimes lose track of the notion that they are learning important concepts about how to become better readers.

Teaching Points

Make Sure the Students Know That the Scattered Clues Strategy Lesson Is a Reading Lesson (and Not Merely a Fun Game to Do in Class)

I start each Scattered Clues Reading Strategy lesson by using one of my actual students (with her permission) as the day's "reader." I invent her story as I do the lesson. I say that my student, Bianca, is reading a *Magic Tree House* book at home and understands everything until she gets to page 43, and then things stop making sense to her. Instead of getting upset as she used to do, Bianca does what she has been taught in this class—she calmly rereads what she does understand, reads the hard-to-understand part again, makes three sensible predictions about the unknown, then keeps reading to hunt for more clues. When she has found enough clues to make a decision, Bianca tells herself what the unknown part probably means.

I always do this sort of storytelling alongside the Scattered Clues Reading Strategy lesson because the story helps students have a much deeper understanding of the crucial teaching points that come out of these lessons.

The Scattered Clues Reading Strategy lessons teach students tricks that mature readers already know about the most effective ways to figure out the author's probable meaning. Most important are these:

Helping Students Internalize the Process of Searching for Meaning

Teachers often know the children *saw* the information, could *understand* the information, but for some weird reason, *chose not to think about the information*. These readers are not trying to understand what they are "reading," and so they do not have a concept of what a clue is or how to use clues. A teacher's exhorting them to use the information that is in the text will be less effective than training them, systematically, to look for clues within the text to confirm or challenge their developing understanding. Through practice with increasingly difficult levels of Scattered Clues Reading Strategy lessons, the students will internalize the process and begin to do it naturally, without repeated exhortations.

Say "Good-bye" to Predictions That No Longer Make Sense

Teachers often find themselves asking kids, "How can you say that when the writing says something completely different?" Children fall in love with their first few predictions, and do not want to give them up. In fact, they are so in love with their initial predictions that they have already imagined whole scenarios, so when the author's next clues invalidate those scenarios, the child just does not want to give them up.

Great readers are relaxed about saying, "Good-bye, prediction!" when a clue suggests a prior prediction no longer makes any sense. They are relaxed about eliminating a prediction because they know they are capable of generating many new predictions any time they get new information. Great readers, therefore, do not have to hold on for dear life to their first three predictions.

> Say "good-bye" to predictions that no longer make sense.

Developing readers, on the other hand, fall in love with their first three predictions. They hold them close to their hearts, and will not say, "Good-bye, prediction!" no matter how unlikely their predictions now seem in light of the new clues. Many ineffective readers know that they are guilty of this nonproductive behavior. They always grin and admit to holding onto contradicted ideas longer than they should. Most would like to know how to stop doing it. If this seems to be the case with your students, teach them to practice waving and saying, "Good-bye, prediction!" as a role-playing activity before you put them through the next Scattered Clues Reading Strategy lesson. Then, when it is time to say good-bye to a prediction, have them wave and say it loud and clear: "Good-bye, prediction!" Each time remind them that, as successful readers, they must be confident that they can always come up with three new predictions any time they want to, so there is no need to hold onto any prediction that no longer makes sense.

Assume the Author Means All of What He Says

Developing readers do sometimes pick and choose which words to pay attention to in the writing. Sometimes they do this because it is easier and quicker than actually struggling over all the information as written and really trying to understand the author too! When children see classroom instruction as a race to the "right answer," even if the teacher does not intend it to be, they sometimes just cherry-pick the easiest-to-understand information, shoot up their hands begging to be called on, and blurt out their first thoughts, hoping that they are making the correct guess. Naturally, nine times out of ten they are wrong. This is a difficult habit for some children to break, especially when they think they're in a race with the entire class to get the teacher's attention and approval.

Fortunately, students want to learn how to read like serious thinkers who contemplate the author's entire idea, but they need some guided practice. Scattered Clues Reading Strategy lessons give students that practice. Teach the child to consider the entire clue, not just parts of a clue, and then to make three predictions. You know when they have considered the entire clue and when they have not by the quality of their predictions.

When the child's predictions indicate that he has used only part of a clue (and he could understand all of the clue, but ignored it), that is the time to point out what he has done, and why, and keep reminding him to "believe the author. Believe that all of these words are what the author means, not just some of them." Then, invite the child to make three different predictions based upon all of the author's language that the child recognizes. The child will be amazed at how smart he is when he considers all of the clues. Keep doing this until the child gives up the habit of choosing words to which he will pay attention and words he will ignore.

Please Don't Say the First Thing That Pops Into Your Head!

"Why are you saying the first thing that pops into your head?!?" Many teachers would like to say this more often to children, but restrain themselves. Educators know the children who habitually say the first thing that occurs to them without pausing for a moment to reflect on whether what they are about to utter makes a bit of sense. Why do these children do that? Most of them think that they have only one shot at getting the "right" answer. They need

to be shown how proficient readers reason their way through print in order to understand. Scattered Clues Reading Strategy lessons help these children learn to make at least three predictions and evaluate each one *before* offering any suggestion to the teacher. I have seen wonderful improvements in children's comprehension and self-esteem when they learn to trust their own intelligence in this manner.

Focus on the Negatives

Teachers often see students ignore such negative terms as *not, no, never, except, however,* and *but.* These children end up with the exact opposite idea of what the author is intending. Why do children do that? Less experienced readers need some practice thinking about negative statements. They are used to thinking about positive statements and so keep doing what they are used to by simply ignoring the negative element in a sentence.

Scattered Clues Reading Strategy lessons can help children consider the implications of a single clue that contains a negative term. If they are having trouble with this, invite them first to think of the positive statement: *Tell yourself what the positive statement means. Got it? Good. Now think of what its opposite could mean.* This way of helping the children understand negation often helps. However, if they choose to ignore the negative portion, their predictions will never make sense within the entire context. This will become pretty obvious after a few lessons. As much as some children really don't want to think that hard about text, they generally concede that they must reconsider and think about the clue containing the negative statement in order to understand the author.

Complex Sentences Contain a Lot of Clues

Teachers know that only their best, most experienced readers unravel the entire meaning in complex sentences. If, for example, a complex sentence has three separate ideas, then these attentive readers can articulate the three ideas. The other students generally can articulate the one idea in the sentence that is easiest to understand. Sometimes the idea they notice is at the beginning or at the very end of a long complex sentence.

What developing readers have to learn is that each idea in a long and complicated sentence is a separate clue! Inexperienced readers need a lot of help with learning to understand the several ideas embedded in a complex sentence. A Scattered Clues Reading Strategy lesson that contains such a sentence offers students an opportunity to begin to learn why it is important to focus on each idea contained therein. If the student can identify each idea in the lengthy clue, then she stands a very good chance of figuring out what the author probably means. However, if the child decides to ignore parts of the long sentence, then she will never be able to figure out the author's meaning. Scattered Clues Reading Strategy lessons help students see why they have to do the hard work of understanding each part of a complex sentence, but that is not enough. These children also have to learn how to take apart complex sentences, and how to create them. The Unraveling Reading Strategy, which is covered in Chapter 8, will help with this.

Frequently Asked Questions

1. When should a teacher step in to guide the thinking of the students?

Never try to lead a student to the best possible answers. Every time you step in to "help" the student get to more sensible answers, you are also preventing the student from thinking of likely possibilities on his own. Thinking of likely possibilities on one's own is what proficient readers do—and thinking of likely possibilities on one's own is the point of the Scattered Clues Reading Strategy lessons. Instead, keep guiding the student to test his predictions in the lesson, saying each prediction out loud with the entire set of clues he sees so far, and then judging whether it still makes sense in light of all the clues provided. Most of the time, the reader will realize on his own that while his prediction made sense with the first clue, it makes no sense at all in light of the second or the third clue.

2. But aren't there students who never realize that their predictions do not make sense with the clues?

Yes. And these situations are choice teaching moments for those kinds of readers. There are always a few students who for one reason or another ignore bits and pieces of clues that they would easily understand if they tried to. When this happens to a reader regularly, I know she needs to take a closer look at the context, so I ask her to defend her choices. For example, a student named Marla completed a Scattered Clues Reading Strategy lesson in this way:

My family and I went to the *supermarket* on Saturday.

I stood in line to get the best seats.

The third clue has not been shown yet. But this reader does not indicate that *supermarket* does not seem to make sense with *get the best seats*. (The other children notice this incongruity, but they know not to say anything while Marla is trying to figure this out.)

So I ask her, "Marla, in your experience, do families usually stand in line to get the best seats at *supermarkets*?" I show no judgment in the tone of my question or in my facial expressions. I wait to hear what she has to say. She thinks . . . then comes the light "No, I guess not."

"So why would you keep *supermarket* as a possible meaning for the first sentence?"

She is not sure.

This is my opportunity to ask her if sometimes she pays attention to only some parts of a clue and not to other parts. In response to my questioning, she agrees that she does this often. When I ask her why, she tells me that she just wants to get to the end of it and be finished.

I explain that this is the difference between reading effectively and not reading effectively: an accomplished reader carefully thinks about the meaning of every sentence, and every part of every sentence, because she wants to understand the author. Instead of speeding to the end, the thoughtful reader takes her time and thinks about the ideas. Many of my students have sheepishly admitted to me and each other that sometimes all they really do is *blah, blah, blah* the words in their heads just to get finished. When I ask Marla if this is what she is doing when she is "reading" something she does not want to read, she grins. It may take a few more sessions of asking Marla to defend her choices, but eventually she will begin to monitor her own choices in terms of whether or not they make sense with all of the ideas.

3. **Why do you say that the Scattered Clues Strategy lessons model the reading process like no other strategy lesson you know of?**

No matter what a proficient reader is trying to understand while reading, the process is always the same. When reading fiction, the proficient reader hunts for clues to the story elements (character, setting, plot, events, theme) and refines his understanding of each element as new clues are revealed. When reading information, the proficient reader hunts for clues to the author's main points and reasons. Again, the reader refines his understanding as he reads through the text. No matter what one reads, the process is always the same: to search actively for sensible meaning from clues.

chapter 5

If You Can Say It in Your Own Words

The Paraphrasing Reading Strategy

Marcus is still reading material at his comfort level, but too often, he misses the important points in the text. Perhaps Marcus knows what happens in a story, but he rarely understands why. Likewise, Marcus might understand bits and pieces of informational text at his level, but he is rarely able to cite the author's major points. It could be that Marcus is not really reading; instead he may be merely saying the words in his head (as rapidly as possible in order to "finish").

When to Teach the Paraphrasing Reading Strategy

Marcus might benefit greatly from being taught how to paraphrase the meaning of every sentence consciously as he "reads." You will know if paraphrasing lessons are called for, if you do the following: Let Marcus try to paraphrase a sentence after reading it silently once or twice. If his understanding is sketchy, invite Marcus to read the same sentence several more times and ask him to try to imagine its meaning as well. If his understanding is much better, then Marcus would probably benefit from learning to paraphrase every sentence as precisely as possible with fairly simple text until it becomes a habit.

How to Teach the Paraphrasing Reading Strategy

The proficient reader continuously tells himself what the author means while reading. When he recalls the text, he recalls how he interpreted the text and rarely recalls the author's actual written language. In, *Ken Goodman on Reading*, Dr. Goodman puts it this way: "But it isn't the text that the reader is making sense of. The reader constructs his or her own text, parallel to the published text, while transacting with it." He goes on to state, "The reading process focuses on this parallel, personally constructed reader text . . ."

In this book, when we say "paraphrase," we mean putting the words of someone else into your own words. We believe that the ability to paraphrase accurately is the essence of comprehension.

Paraphrasing is what readers do to test their comprehension. There is no comprehension if one is unable to paraphrase all or part of what the author has said. Proficient readers try to paraphrase the author's written language any time they come to a challenging section of text. When finished reading, the proficient reader recalls her paraphrases for the most part and only a little of the author's actual written language. Unfortunately, many developing readers don't bother to paraphrase much. Instead, they say the author's words very quickly and paraphrase only those parts they cannot avoid understanding.

Paraphrasing Reading Strategy lessons put readers through the process of articulating the author's written language as precisely as possible. At times, developing readers will have gaps in their understanding because they lack some prior knowledge. But wherever the developing reader can understand, she will be challenged to interpret the author's specific ideas in her own words.

> If you can say it accurately in your own words, you understand it.

Paraphrase—a restatement of a text, passage, or work giving the meaning in another form

Comprehension— the act of grasping meaning with the intellect

After a section of text has been paraphrased, the reader will also be asked to summarize the information she has understood so far, and cautioned not to skip anything. Young readers often enjoy the challenge. It also has the desired result of making developing readers very attentive to the ideas conveyed in written language. In other words, Paraphrasing Reading Strategy lessons give developing readers the necessary practice of telling themselves the meaning of every single idea that they can understand.

What Is Different About Paraphrasing Reading Strategy Lessons?

Paraphrasing Reading Strategy lessons are different from all other lessons in this book. There are no pre-made lessons. Instead, these lessons follow a procedure you will go through with authentic text. The lessons are best taught in small groups of four students who work in pairs. The group of four students should read at about the same level. The group chooses the book they will read. This is essential. They must be interested in understanding the ideas or they will not really try to paraphrase. The group pores over a bunch of likely books that are at their level and then decides what to read for the next few days.

First, everyone reads the page silently. Then one student volunteers to say the words of the page or a paragraph aloud. Her partner paraphrases the writing in his own words without looking at the print. The other pair listens, and they have a chance to comment later about whether or not the ideas were paraphrased correctly and completely.

Materials to Use for Paraphrasing Reading Strategy

For practicing paraphrasing, leveled guided reading booklets are very useful, whether fiction or nonfiction. Surprisingly, children seem to learn paraphrasing faster with informational texts. Informational texts have a lot of specific information that the attentive reader will naturally attempt to explain to him- or herself; therefore, such texts are perfect for this kind of exercise.

Students' Roles During Paraphrasing Reading Strategy Lessons

All students volunteer for their roles as either the "sayer of words" or the "explainer of ideas." Most young readers love to say the words aloud. They call this "reading." So in this exercise, one child has the joyful task of saying the words aloud. The student who struggles with naming words will usually volunteer to explain the ideas initially. The student who reads a lot, knows reading is about understanding, and is confident in her ability to understand what she reads also generally volunteers to explain the ideas. Most of the other students volunteer to say the words aloud. All students eventually get to do both roles.

Procedures for Conducting Paraphrasing Reading Strategy Lessons in Groups of Four

♦ Each student has the same book in her hands. The teacher asks, "Who would like to say the words?" Most hands shoot up. The teacher picks one person. The teacher then asks, "Who would like to explain the ideas?" Initially, it is usually the case that only one person raises his hand, in a tentative fashion.

♦ To get the ball rolling, the teacher becomes the "explainer of ideas" and everyone else is the "sayer of words." The group works on one page at a time. They look at the picture clues of the first page. Based upon these clues, they make three predictions about what the writing might say in precise terms. They then predict the language the author might use to represent each idea, which is a good way to prepare students to understand any author.

♦ The first "sayer of words" pronounces the words on the first page. The teacher asks the "sayer" to say them again, and then again, so the others have enough repetition to begin to focus on the ideas. Then the teacher explains most of the ideas in her own words and leaves one of the ideas for a volunteering student to paraphrase.

♦ Repeat this procedure for three more pages, so that each student has had an opportunity to "say the words." (The same student may be the only one to volunteer to explain some of the page.) After the fourth page, the learners have begun to understand what it means to "explain the ideas."

♦ The teacher steps out of the role of "explainer" and invites a student to do it.

♦ A student who has strong comprehension abilities is chosen as the "explainer."

♦ A child who has strong word-calling abilities becomes the "sayer of words."

♦ The remaining two students will either agree or add information the "explainer" may have forgotten to mention.

It is very important that the person saying the words is not also the explainer (or paraphraser) of the ideas, for several reasons. First, most developing readers cannot pay attention to the ideas when they are saying words aloud. They are far too concerned with just saying the words accurately. Second, most developing readers are not used to paying attention to the minute details of each written idea. Therefore, they need quiet, patience, and sometimes repetition in order to interpret the written language in their own words.

Often, at the beginning of these lessons, the "explainer of ideas" will ask the "sayer of words" to please say the words again, and maybe even again. Why? Even though the "explainer" is looking at the words while they are being said aloud, she is not getting the ideas completely. The ideas are still hazy. So the "sayer" is asked to say the words again. The paraphraser often needs to hear and see the writing two or three times before the author's ideas begin to become clear to her.

The paraphraser is invited to close her eyes and picture the meaning. Then when she is ready, she turns the book upside down so she cannot see the writing, and says all the meaning in her own words without forgetting anything. The second pair of students judges whether all ideas were paraphrased. Once that is done, the second pair of students becomes the "sayer of words" and the "explainer of ideas" with a new section of text.

Throughout this procedure, the teacher asks the group, "Who is reading, the 'sayer' or the 'explainer'?" At the start of these lessons, the students will be confident that the "sayer of words" is the reader. But, after many experiences of struggling to articulate the ideas, these students begin to realize that both the "sayer" and the "explainer" are "reading" because both are trying to understand the author's probable meaning. The harder job is to explain the author's ideas.

Teaching Points

Initially, it is beneficial to have students consciously try to paraphrase the meaning of every sentence on the page or in the paragraph—depending upon reading level. First, each student counts the number of sentences on the page. If there are four sentences, then the student will try to remember four ideas. The student reads the first sentence once or twice, covers the sentence, tells himself its meaning, uncovers the sentence, and checks to see if he paraphrased completely. If he has, he repeats the process with the next sentence. If he has not recalled correctly, he rereads the first sentence and tries to get it all this time. When he has paraphrased all four sentences, he covers the page and tries to tell himself all four ideas. All the students in the class who have been conducting the same exercise with the same material come together and say what they remember. They are usually very proud of their improved understanding of text. Students can also be paired to help each other do this process before doing it by themselves.

Accept That Prior Knowledge Affects What Students Can Understand

At some point during paraphrasing lessons, students will be stymied. They will have almost no understanding of the text. No matter which reading trick they try to use, no matter how assiduously they try to apply it, they cannot really get a handle on what the author means. The best these maturing readers can do is to make very general inferences that "this section has something to do with x, y, and z, but I don't know what x, y, and z are!" This is the moment when the teacher can reassure students about a fundamental truth of reading: "A reader's prior knowledge limits what that reader can understand." While children know this truth already, it is reassuring to them to hear you say it, and say it often.

Apply Previously Taught Reading Strategies

Paraphrasing Reading Strategy lessons requires students to interpret the text as precisely as possible. During these sessions, the learners will have many opportunities to practice applying all of the tricks they have learned from previously taught reading strategy lessons. Students will gain skill in applying reading strategies more proficiently during these sessions.

Before starting practice sessions in applying previously taught strategies, you must first introduce a behavior we call "Freeze." You must teach the group how to remain neutral and nonreactive in expression no matter what is said when you ask them to "Freeze!" Everyone sits with hands clasped on the table, and patiently waits for the reader to apply a reading strategy. It is amazing how cooperative everyone is. Few students ever give away the word if they know it. Students love to do "Freeze."

The "sayer of words" is the person responsible for applying the cloze and nicknaming strategies. When the "sayer of words" runs into a word that she does not recognize, wait for the student to automatically apply a proficient reading strategy. If she does not, this is a teaching moment. Ask everyone to "Freeze!" Everyone is quiet and patient; no one moves. No one gives any hints verbally or through body language.

Depending upon the problem blocking the student, the teacher will guide him in applying one of the reading strategies described earlier.

Cloze Strategy: If the "sayer" comes to an unfamiliar word and does not know how to deal with it in order to understand the author, the teacher will guide this student in applying the strategy. The "sayer" must do what she has been taught during Cloze Reading Strategy lessons:

♦ Get to the end of the sentence containing the mysterious word.

♦ Go back to the beginning of that sentence and repeat the entire sentence again, saying "hum" over the unknown word.

♦ Say the sentence three times in that manner.

♦ Ask, "What could this mean that would make sense to me?"

♦ Make three logical predictions.

If more information is needed, direct the "sayer" to start earlier in the paragraph when everything made more sense to her, then do the cloze steps again, remembering to read past the unknown word by a few sentences. Once the meaning of the unfamiliar words has been decided, the "explainer" can paraphrase the author's ideas.

Nicknaming Reading Strategy: If the "sayer" comes to unpronounceable proper nouns and does not know how to deal with them in order to understand the author, the teacher guides the student in applying the Nicknaming Reading Strategy.

The "sayer" must do what she has been taught during the Nicknaming Reading Strategy lessons:

♦ Call the unknown names by their first letter.

♦ Say the entire sentence three times.

♦ Make three predications about what the nickname may represent in the text.

As more pages are read later on, more information will be forthcoming about the role of these nicknames. Eventually, one of the "explainers" will have to decide what each proper noun's function might be. Once the possible functions of the proper nouns have been decided, the "explainer" can paraphrase the author's ideas.

Recognize that Paraphrasing Can Provide a Breakthrough Opportunity for Students Who Struggle with Words

Once the least able "sayer of words" knows how to figure out the meaning of unfamiliar words and names, she becomes ready to "say the words aloud" too. But this miracle does not happen automatically or quickly. Instead, it happens because the student who initially struggles with words learns how to apply the Cloze and Nicknaming Strategies *during these exercises*. Until now, the reader who struggles with words has steadfastly refused to employ either the Cloze or the Nicknaming Strategy. She believes strongly that she must name every word correctly, and she struggles mightily to do just that.

Now the student who has struggled with words has gained confidence in her ability to explain the ideas if the words are said aloud. She has been doing that well for weeks during the paraphrasing lessons. Also, she has watched more able students repeatedly employ Cloze Reading Strategy to either name the unfamiliar words or name their meanings successfully. This student has also watched more able students unashamedly nickname proper nouns by their first letters and keep going. It has been apparent to her that these students have benefited from the nicknaming because they understand the ideas better.

Eventually the student who can understand when something is read to her but who struggles with words on her own will decide to try to use the Cloze or Nicknaming Reading Strategy. The minute she finds she can figure out the meaning of many words and functions of proper nouns on her own, without help, this learner begins to believe she can learn to read well. When she finally makes the decision to try to understand the ideas, instead of merely saying all the words accurately, she also makes the decision to begin to read proficiently.

Application of proficient reading strategies during paraphrasing sessions liberates many kinds of struggling readers from the mystery of written language and enables them to begin to enjoy higher levels of reading comprehension.

Frequently Asked Questions

1. **Don't all readers automatically paraphrase whatever they read when they find the text challenging? Why does it have to be taught?**

   No. All readers do not automatically paraphrase whenever they read challenging material. Proficient readers do, and when they don't, they know it. They stop reading and go back to wherever they started to encounter difficulties to get back into the text and reread.

   Developing readers with less effective reading strategies will sometimes paraphrase when the meaning is inescapable, and sometimes they will not—especially when they just want to finish. In those instances, a remarkable event happens that so many teachers have observed repeatedly: the student says all the words fluently, and even with expression, but has little idea what the writing was about. These readers need to know that it is their responsibility to tell themselves the meaning of what they are reading as they are reading, as proficient readers do.

2. **Why aren't there reproducible strategy lessons for paraphrasing like the ones you have for other strategy lessons?**

   Paraphrasing is a reading decision and the quality of each student's paraphrase depends on her prior knowledge. It's important to give developing readers who do not automatically paraphrase whenever they are challenged by what they are reading ample opportunities in class to do so. There is no reproducible that I can think of that takes the place of inviting readers to articulate what they understand as precisely as possible.

3. **What is the difference between paraphrasing and summarizing?**

   Readers paraphrase every bit of language they see; that is, they restate it to themselves in another form. It is an ongoing mental process. Summarizing is a shortened version of paraphrasing. It is a decision to reduce all the information the reader has understood to a brief statement of the essential ideas.

4. Does teaching paraphrasing help older students understand more of what they read? Does it have anything to do with study skills?

There are several other ways to generate paraphrases from older students. One way is by teaching students to write margin notes. Of course, we don't want students to write in public school textbooks, but you can photocopy sample informational texts so that there are enlarged margins. Then show students how to paraphrase in writing the meaning of each and every paragraph. Sticky notes also work well for this. Students can jot down their "paraphrasing" on a sticky note and attach it to the page next to the paragraph. Afterward, students find it much easier to summarize the main points. Older students really appreciate learning this study skill trick, especially when they feel they are confronted with pages and pages of text. The main point is that older readers are not necessarily proficient readers, and they, too, may have to learn effective reading strategies like paraphrasing the material they have to read.

chapter 6

What If I Don't Recognize Half the Words? Can I Understand Anything?

The Nonsense Reading Strategy

Shakira is trying to understand informational texts that have an abundance of unfamiliar content words. There are so many, in fact, that she usually gives up and does not try to understand anything. For example, let us say that Shakira has been assigned to read a science text that contains this sentence: "All molecules are made from atoms." Maybe Shakira can pronounce *molecules* and *atoms*, and maybe she cannot, but the bottom line is that she does not know what either an *atom* or a *molecule* is. More important, Shakira has no useful strategy to help her get even a glimmer of the text's meaning. Shakira is an ineffective reader, so she understands almost nothing and gives up quickly.

When to Teach the Nonsense Reading Strategy

Like Shakira, if one of your students interacts with informational texts that contain many unfamiliar words and concepts, he or she would benefit from Nonsense Reading Strategy lessons. These lessons show students how to pay attention to the connective language, especially words such as *both, except, however, if . . . then*. These words are very useful. They show how unfamiliar content words are related to or different from one another. If students were taught to employ the Nonsense Reading Strategy, they would figure out that *atoms* (whatever they are) make up *molecules* (whatever they are). This happens to be a crucial understanding in the field of chemistry. They would also know to try and find understandable reference books, perhaps in the children's or junior section of the library, in order to develop a more complete idea of the meaning of *atoms* and *molecules*.

Focusing Students on the Meaning of Adverbs and Connective Language

A related strategy that Shakira—and some of your students—may need is to be sure to tell themselves the meaning of words such as *always, sometimes,* and *never.* Informational texts are often organized to show how items are similar and different by using such qualifying terms as *often, always, sometimes,* and *never*. If students do not notice and paraphrase these words usefully, they would benefit from lessons that ask them to do so in text they can easily understand. Nonsense Reading Strategy lessons help students learn to do this.

How to Teach the Nonsense Reading Strategy

Nonsense Reading Strategy lessons help learners who are overwhelmed by unfamiliar words learn to use adverbs, connective language, and their knowledge of English syntax to infer how unknowns are related to one another. This strategy is employed by good readers when reading challenging informational texts, textbooks, and standardized reading tests.

Nonsense Reading Strategy lessons are composed of three to five sentences in a paragraph, followed by three to five comprehension-type questions. The sentences in the paragraph contain many nonsense words that are connected by such function words as *the, that, a, in, on, of, by, have, many, as, but, only, however, until, when, is, are, it, they, both, except, often, sometimes, never,* and so on.

> A large number of the words in any text are function words, including prepositions, conjunctions, auxiliary verbs, determiners, and pronouns.

The proficient reader pays attention to these words to determine how the content-specific words might be related to one another. But the developing reader often ignores the function words and continues to worry about saying the content-specific words correctly even though these words are completely alien to the reader and, in themselves, convey incomplete meaning at best.

Comprehension-type questions follow each paragraph. They can be literal or inferential. The easier lessons are mainly literal. The more difficult lessons are mostly inferential. The comprehension questions can be answered correctly if the reader uses her knowledge of English syntax and if she uses logic. However, if the reader does not pay close attention to the "function language" and does not treat these words as clues, she may not be able to answer the questions or to comprehend the text.

Sample Nonsense Reading Strategy Lessons

The Nonsense Reading Strategy lesson imitates what proficient readers do when confronted with several unfamiliar content-bearing words in one sentence. The reader hunts for clues to the sentence's meaning from the connective language and the sentence's syntax. For example, this simple Nonsense lesson highlights the connective language.

Lesson #1

Example 1

The blixer was blixing in the smetnen. It was very helpful. The blixer was rospented in 1806.

1. Where was the blixer blixing?
    a. in the smetnen
    b. in the broster

2. When was the blixer rospented?
    a. in 2006
    b. in 1806

3. Is the blixer
    a. a good thing? Why?
    b. a bad thing? Why?

The following more complicated Nonsense lesson imitates typical textbook sentences. It highlights the kinds of connective language, such as *however* and *both*, often ignored by developing readers.

Example 2

Both the Meldot and the Bonpel complent. They exuset by the desanin. However, only the Meldot can exuset without a toolel.

1. What do the Meldot and the Bonpel do the same?
    a. toolel
    b. complent

2. What is different about the Meldot?
    a. the complent
    b. It can exuset without a toolel.

3. Does the Bonpel probably need a toolel to exuset?
    a. Yes. Why?
    b. No. Why?

How to Construct Nonsense Reading Strategy Lessons

In beginning lessons with this strategy, use only one easy-to-pronounce nonsense word to stand for every content-bearing word in the three- or four-sentence paragraph. Too many nonsense words distract the students who are focused primarily on sounding out words. Use simple sentences and mostly literal comprehension-style questions. Include one inference question to illustrate the power of connective language to unveil complicated relationships.

In more difficult lessons, use a wide variety of nonsense words to stand for meaningful ideas. The reader will have to infer how each of the nonsense words is related to the others, as well as infer other possible meanings.

Possible Topics for Nonsense Reading Strategy Lessons

♦ Imitations of informational texts

♦ Imitations of essays, contracts, directions, and other common nonfiction formats

Creating Nonsense Reading Strategy Lessons From Texts

Start with material that students must read in class, such as kids' magazines, textbooks, and newspapers. Pick a paragraph or two from one, and create a few comprehension-style questions that can be figured out using logic and attention to connective language.

With more proficient readers, use advanced texts such as adult encyclopedias and science texts. Pick a paragraph. Create a few comprehension-style questions. Let the children work together to apply logic to figure out the answers.

Test Preparation

Give the students standardized reading, science, and history test examples to which they can apply the Nonsense Reading Strategy. Mastering this application will give them a new and powerful strategy for scoring higher on such tests.

Teaching Points

♦ *But I can't read this! It has too many words I don't know!* Children often think this and sometimes say it out loud when confronted with very challenging texts about unfamiliar topics. What these children don't realize is that they can, in fact, pull substantial information from these texts. This is a very important insight that proficient readers have and that developing readers lack.

Proficient readers are not fazed by unfamiliar topics. If, for some reason, such texts are required reading, proficient readers will try to eke out some useful bits of meaning. They will focus on the function words, relational and connective language, and the syntax of the sentences; and they employ logic in order to understand some of the text.

♦ *Why didn't you pay attention to the little words?* Teachers often want to ask this of some of their students. They know that many children do not bother to pay attention to the function words—sometimes called the "little words," although not all of them are short—and thus, misunderstand the author's meaning. Once the nonsense lessons are completed, developing readers will have a new respect for the "little words." They will begin to pay close attention to them. They will use these function words as guides to the author's meaning. Initially, developing readers may even pay more attention to the connective language than to the content-bearing words. Later, they will give all clues equal weight, and function words will be included in the readers' minds as clues.

♦ *Don't be afraid of standardized reading tests. Just get used to using logic to figure out the answers. It often doesn't matter that you know nothing about the topic. You can still score well.* Teachers and proficient young readers know this truth, but developing readers do not believe it. They think that if they don't know all the words, they cannot understand a single thing in the test. The nonsense lessons will disabuse them of this belief.

Once students have experienced a few of these lessons, give them actual sample reading tests to show them how much better they can score if they use the strategy. This will convince even the doubters as nothing else can.

Frequently Asked Questions

1. **Don't all readers pay attention to the connective language in sentences? After all, they have been able to read those kinds of words for years. Why wouldn't they pay attention to them?**

   When developing readers begin to try to understand advanced text, their attention is often so riveted on the unfamiliar words that the familiar function words seem unhelpful by comparison. Developing readers mistakenly discount the importance of words such as *both, not, never, with, on, in, however, some, all*, and so on. But experience has taught proficient readers that these words are lifelines to their comprehension and may be the only things that they do understand when so much of what is on the page seems meaningless.

2. **If so much of the advanced text is meaningless to the reader, what do you tell students to do to catch on to relationships among all those unfamiliar terms?**

   I tell them to do what I did when I used to read chemistry textbooks. I would call every meaningful word by its first letter in order to see the sentence's meaning more clearly.

   So this humdinger:

   Both the Meldot and the Bonpel complent. They exuset by the desanin. However, only the Meldot can exuset without a toolel.

   Would be said:

   Both the M and the B c. They e by the d. However, only the M can e without a t.

3. **Are Nonsense Reading Strategy lessons useful in helping students get ready for standardized reading tests?**

   Definitely. Comprehension questions about passages are often just as hard to understand as the passages themselves, so focusing intently on the connective language in both the passage and the questions helps readers gain an edge in understanding and in choosing the correct answer.

How Do I Know What *That* Means?

The Pronoun Referent Reading Strategy

Bruce is a fourth grader who is reading informational text. The book he is reading is *Training a Guide Dog* (MacDonald, 2000). The print says, "Which dogs are not suitable? It is those dogs that are frightened of noises, busy places, or heavy traffic. These dogs usually become family pets."

Bruce has read this portion of the text a few times silently to try to understand it better. Since he knows how to use the context to infer the meaning of unfamiliar words, Bruce has inferred that *suitable* probably means in this context *ready to be a guide dog*. But Bruce does not know what happens to the dogs who are not suitable. Why doesn't he know that? The text seems clear.

When I suggest to Bruce that he substitute *not suitable* for *these*, Bruce now gets the sentence: "Oh, dogs that are not suitable become family pets!"

Why Teach the Pronoun Referent Reading Strategy

More than likely, Bruce had "said" the pronoun in his head. He had said *these* in his head, but Bruce did not tell himself what the pronoun meant in this context. This problem occurs fairly often when Bruce—and many other developing readers—are reading. It is a major reason why some students frequently have trouble inferring meaning from texts containing an abundance of pronouns. The Pronoun Referent Reading Strategy addresses this problem and helps such readers learn to figure out to what the pronoun is probably referring.

How to Teach the Pronoun Referent Reading Strategy

The Pronoun Referent Reading Strategy is used by proficient readers when they tell themselves what each pronoun probably stands for as they are reading. If the reader is unsure, he may reread the preceding text or just rethink the question, "To what word is this pronoun probably referring?" The Pronoun Referent Reading Strategy lesson will help Bruce to infer the probable meanings of the pronouns he sees. These lessons will improve his comprehension of informational texts especially.

Oral Language Practice With Pronoun Referents

Before presenting written exercises or strategy lessons, I have found it useful to begin showing children that they already know how to identify the meaning of pronouns when they talk to one another. I start by giving my student Susan a box of tissues, and then ask her, "Would you give *it* to Bruce who is sitting next to you?" Which, of course, she does. Then I ask what *it* meant. All students know the answer: the box of tissues! Next, I might ask Bruce to give *it* back to *her,* which he does. I ask what *her* means, and they reply, as a chorus, "Susan!"

I find using oral examples helps my students to see that they already know how to understand the meaning of pronouns when they converse. I explain how writing is similar to talking. When we talk, there are so many ways we understand the pronoun: by our facial expressions, body movements, tone, and many other cues. When reading, we have fewer cues to help us. In order to decide the likely meaning of a pronoun, a reader often has to re-read or rethink the sentences preceding the pronoun. This oral introduction to inferring the meaning of pronouns seems to help students view this as an everyday sort of activity instead of rocket science.

Using Guided Reading Books

Here is the first trick I teach my students when they have trouble understanding what the pronoun in a text means. I advise them to ask themselves a question about the not-yet-related pronoun and its unidentified referent. For example, the questions might be "What *they*?" "What *it*?" What *this*?" I then encourage them to read the sentences that come just before the unrelated pronoun to try to answer their own question and identify the most likely referent.

In practicing the Pronoun Referent Reading Strategy with your students, choose reading material that is fairly easy for them to understand—books about topics that interest them. So, for example, in the book *Training a Guide Dog*, the text says: "I housebreak the puppy. This is very important because. . ." I teach my students to ask themselves, "What is *this*?" "What do I know about *this*?" They will respond that "*This* is very important." Then I ask, "*What* is very important?" and I remind them to reread the preceding text. Soon many students realize what *this* represents: h*ousebreaking the puppy.*

Here is another example. When *Training a Guide Dog* says, "It takes about five months to train a guide dog. At the end of that time, the dog is ready to meet its new owner," I take the students through the same process. They ask, "At the end of *what* time?" and look at the preceding text. "Oh, at the end of five months the dog is ready!" say my newly enlightened students proudly.

Sometimes asking themselves what the pronoun means in a given context does not help. Then, I take the next step. I let my students write several possible predictions on photocopied pages of the guided reading book. I advise them that it helps their understanding if they try to be as precise as possible when writing their predictions. After writing several possibilities, they are to pick the one prediction that seems to make the most sense with the rest of the text.

For example, when the text says, "We visit busy places so that the puppy can become used to noise and being with people," Bruce's three predictions were that "We" means:

1. The girl (in the picture, buying fruit), the woman (in the picture, holding the dog's leash), and the dog

2. The woman and the dog

3. The guide dog puppy trainer and the guide dog puppy.

Reading further, Bruce decides his third prediction makes the most sense because the text that follows says: "I always put this special coat on the puppy when we [the guide dog puppy trainer and the guide dog puppy] are walking. This lets people know that the puppy is in training." Everything seems to go together well using this prediction. Please note that although pronouns almost always refer back to something that came earlier in the text, reading ahead a bit can also help to confirm or eliminate a prediction made by the reader.

Teaching Points

When a student figures out the meaning of pronouns on her own, without help or hints from the teacher, she gains confidence as well as an understanding of how to approach complex sentences.

Dos and Don'ts of Pronoun Referent Reading Strategy Lessons

♦ **Do elicit three or more logical predictions about the meaning of a pronoun. But don't give the student any extra hints or help of any kind, no matter how tempting.** The student is on her own with the text. The only strategy she should be taught is to make three logical predictions regarding what the pronoun might mean. Then guide the student to substitute each prediction into the sentence and ask herself, "Does this really make sense to me?" If the answer is "No," then direct the student to try her second prediction and ask again, "Does this sentence make sense to me now?" If the answer is still "No," suggest the student insert her third prediction, and ask herself, "Does this now make sense in the sentence and with the surrounding sentences, too?" The third logical prediction often works. When a student is not used to thinking of more than one possibility, she often finds that three or even four logical predictions will lead to something that makes sense in the context. Figuring out the right pronoun on her own builds her confidence.

♦ **Do teach students to write the possible meaning of the referent above the pronoun and read the entire paragraph using that meaning to judge whether it makes sense.** If it does not, write the second prediction above the pronoun, read the entire paragraph to see if it makes sense now, and so on. This trick of writing the name of the referent above the pronoun is very useful for developing readers who don't yet understand how to deal with referents. Remind students that when reading an actual textbook or library book they should write on sticky notes.

♦ **Do show children some of the fundamental rules of figuring out the meaning of referents.** Within one paragraph, often the thing (noun) mentioned in the preceding sentence is the meaning of the pronoun in the subsequent sentence. It is the reader's job to substitute the noun for the pronoun and decide logically what the pronoun means. It helps learners to use arrows and underlining to point to the nouns to which the pronouns refer.

Within one paragraph, an entire phrase mentioned in a preceding sentence can be the meaning of the pronoun in a subsequent sentence. The reader has to insert various printed phrases to decide which phrase the pronoun probably means. Again, it helps learners to use arrows and underlining to point to the nouns to which the pronouns refer.

Often a pronoun in the first sentence of a paragraph refers to a noun contained in the final sentence of the preceding paragraph. Show students how this happens with authentic, familiar texts such as the class novel or informational texts.

Frequently Asked Questions

1. Are you telling me that some readers do not automatically infer what the pronouns refer to in written language? I thought they did know because students absolutely do understand pronouns when they are used in conversation.

Written language has its own conventions that are similar to, but different from, spoken language. Spoken language has the advantage of gestures, tone, and back-and-forth conversation—all of which help to provide additional information. Written language does not have these real-time communication advantages, so the reader has to know and understand how pronoun referents work in written language to understand the author well. Proficient readers have figured out most of these conventions, but developing readers seem to understand the pronouns in context primarily when the meaning is inescapable. Pronoun Referent Reading Strategy lessons help to make clear to developing readers how pronouns work in written language, especially informational text.

2. Why do you say that Pronoun Referent Reading Strategy lessons are particularly useful for understanding informational text?

Many expositions start with a basic idea expressed explicitly, followed by supporting details that contain many pronouns referring to the first explicit idea in some way. My students count the number of pronouns in the first paragraph of an article and note where the pronouns are located and what type is used most often. They exclaim, "Here is a *this*!" "Here is a *her*!" "What does *that* mean in this article?" and so on. My students begin to notice the different pronouns and how frequently they appear in the text they are examining. If they practice enough, they begin to understand where they might expect to see pronouns in texts and why they are used. At the very least, students are attuned to spotting pronouns and to regarding them as words having real meaning that they can often figure out.

3. When a developing reader is uncertain of the meaning of a pronoun, does it affect his ability to comprehend?

Absolutely. I have found that when a student is unsure what the writing is about, it is often due to his not being certain about what the pronouns refer to. So I invite the student to identify as precisely as possible what he thinks each pronoun might mean. His inferences help me understand whether or not one or more of the pronouns' meanings is unclear to him.

4. What is the most difficult kind of pronoun referent for developing readers?

The most difficult kind of pronoun to understand is one that refers to an idea contained in an earlier clause, phrase, sentence, or entire paragraph. Students need lots of practice inserting whole phrases in the place of the pronoun to decide whether that phrase is what the author might mean.

These Sentences Are Too Long!

The Unraveling Reading Strategy

Rashad, an eighth grader, can paraphrase the meaning of simple sentences but seems to get lost when reading longer and more complex sentences. Rashad does not understand why authors combine sentences into longer ones, and he does not know the various tricks authors use to make complex sentences. Rashad would benefit from strategy lessons that help him infer what long and complex sentences mean.

When to Teach the Unraveling Reading Strategy

Probably the greatest obstacle to comprehension for Rashad, and even for more able readers, is the complex sentence. Understanding all the ideas embedded within a complex sentence remains a challenge even for quite proficient readers. The more able reader may know well how to understand clues provided in simple sentences but may be stymied when confronted with long, complex sentences with many pronouns and referents. Social studies, math, science, health, and technology textbooks, to name a few, rely on complex sentences to convey their ideas quickly and without redundancy. If a reader does not know how to deal effectively with complex sentences, he will have a great deal of trouble understanding his textbooks and research materials. And the trouble will only get worse as he ascends through the grades. College texts are replete with 50-word sentences. I recommend that all students be taught the Unraveling Reading Strategy when they begin to struggle with understanding complex sentences.

How to Teach the Unraveling Reading Strategy

Research has repeatedly found that a reader's ability to understand and create complex sentences correlates directly to her level of reading comprehension. The greater her ability to create and unravel complex sentences, the greater will be her ability to comprehend complicated text. The purpose of the Unraveling Reading Strategy lessons is to show readers both how to unravel and how to create complex sentences, and how to decide logically what the pronouns within complex sentences stand for. As with all of the reading strategy lessons presented in this book, it is much better if you teach this strategy at a moment when students are struggling with long and complex sentences.

When approaching the subject of complex sentences and how to understand them, I first model how I would break down the sentences my students are struggling with, and then ask whether they would like to learn how to do this. There is always a loud chorus of "Yes! Please!" Even second graders are fascinated by how complex sentences are created and then broken apart. I generally highlight three types of such lessons. The first is breaking long sentences into three- or four-word phrases and imagining the meaning of each chunk. The second is teaching students how to combine a series of simple sentences into a longer, complex sentence. The third, and most difficult for students to understand, is teaching students how to unravel complex sentences into a series of simpler sentences. Through practice with breaking down and building up complex sentences, students begin to feel more comfortable with them, to understand what the connections are within these sentences, and to be more adept at drawing meaning from them.

Teaching How to Break a Long Sentence Into a Series of Shorter Phrases

The first trick, breaking up long sentences into phrases and imagining the meaning of each phrase, would show Rashad how to break up sentences into smaller, more understandable units. Sometimes all that readers have to do to understand a long sentence is to cut it up into smaller, more understandable phrases or clauses. Take, for example, the text in *Training a Guide Dog* that says,

"I housebreak the puppy. This is very important because when the puppy becomes a guide dog and goes into stores and restaurants, it must not make a mess on the floor."

The proficient reader might cut up the second sentence as follows:

♦ First, deal with the pronoun at the start of the second sentence.

♦ "*This* is very important." (What is very important?) The proficient reader looks at the preceding sentence and realizes that *This* probably means *housebreaking the puppy*.

♦ The next step is to consider the meaning of each chunk (phrase) now that the meaning of *This* has become clearer.

♦ Next, our proficient reader will consider the second phrase "because when the puppy becomes a guide dog," and tell himself, "Housebreaking is very important when the puppy becomes a guide dog."

- The third phrase suggests, "Housebreaking is very important when the puppy goes into stores and restaurants."

- The final phrase suggests, "Housebreaking is very important so that the guide dog puppy will not pee on the floors."

The students who I teach often find that if they break apart a long sentence into smaller, more understandable chunks (phrases), they can understand the entire sentence much better than if they try to comprehend the entire long sentence in one go. However, in addition to knowing how to break up long sentences, developing readers also benefit from knowing how to combine shorter sentences to form complex sentences of their own.

Teaching How to Combine Shorter Sentences Into One Longer, Complex Sentence

In my experience, it is better if students have practice creating long sentences before they try to unravel complex sentences. Start by giving your students a lot of practice creating grammatically correct complex sentences. Show them how to use commas and various kinds of pronouns to create a wide variety of complex sentences. The students will begin by learning to combine two sentences, then three sentences, then four or even more. I explain to my students that beginning readers often enjoy reading a lot of short, simple sentences like these:

1. *Ms. Lazar is my reading teacher.*

2. *Ms. Lazar shows me how to read better.*

3. *Ms. Lazar has a class three days a week.*

But proficient readers think reading only short sentences is boring. They would prefer it if the author could find ways to combine the ideas into a single sentence, something like this:

Ms. Lazar, who is my reading teacher, shows me how to read better three times a week.

I invite the students to infer what *who* might mean in this long sentence, keeping in mind that whatever they decide must make sense with the rest of the writing. As they explain, I draw arrows pointing from *who* to *Ms. Lazar.*

Next, the students are given sets of simple sentences about school to combine. Here is another example. This time the pronoun highlighted is *which.*

1. *Our class is going to have a Thanksgiving party.*

2. *I think the Thanksgiving party will be fun.*

The students struggle to decide how to do this. Finally, they think they have it.

*Our class is going to have a Thanksgiving party, **which** I think will be fun.*

As they explain, I draw an arrow from the pronoun *which* to its referent, *Thanksgiving party.*

I point out again that a whole book of simple sentences would become boring for them to read, too. That is why writers find ways to combine simpler sentences. When you begin these lessons, try to stay well within topics and language that are very familiar to your students. With time and practice, the students will become more proficient at sentence combining, but it takes time. It also helps if your students have ample opportunity to study a wide variety of written material. Their inquiry task is to try to infer some of the rules of sentence combining by studying what published authors seem to do.

Here is a much more advanced sample lesson that invites students to use a variety of pronouns effectively to combine sentences. Remember, the more adept students become at combining sentences, the more effectively they will be able understand them while reading. This lesson can be found in the appendix on pages 120 through 126.

Lesson #1

Sentences About Cinderella

Use such words as *who, whom, whose, he, she, this, that, which, those, it,* and *them.* Combine each set of simple sentences into one longer, but equally sensible, sentence.

1a. The fairy tale is about Cinderella.

1b. Cinderella is a young girl.

2a. Cinderella lives with her stepmother and two stepsisters.

2b. The stepmother is cruel and nasty.

3a. Cinderella had to do all the cleaning and washing for the family.

3b. The rest of the family didn't do any work.

(continued on next page)

4a. The Prince was having a party to meet the young ladies.

4b. Cinderella's family was going to the party.

4c. Cinderella was not allowed to go.

5a. Cinderella had only dirty old clothes to wear.

5b. A fairy godmother helped Cinderella go to the party.

6a. Cinderella had to leave the party by midnight.

6b. Cinderella danced with the Prince.

6c. Cinderella ran out of the party at midnight.

6d. Cinderella left her glass shoe at the party.

7a. The Prince looked for Cinderella by having women try on the glass shoe.

7b. Finally, the Prince found Cinderella.

7c. The Prince and Cinderella married.

How to Unravel Complex Sentences Into Their Component Sentences

Once the students can create complex sentences with some ease, address how to unravel complex sentences into their component smaller sentences. Here is an example of an unraveling exercise that is somewhat advanced. You can find it in the appendix on page 117.

How are long sentences made? This long sentence was made with the words *who*, *so that*, and two commas.

The third pig, **who** *was smarter than the other pigs, built his house out of bricks* **so that** *the hungry wolf could not blow it down.* *(26 words)*

> One long sentence can be broken down into several smaller sentences.

What could the word *who* mean in this sentence? Make three predictions! Choose the meaning that seems to make the most sense.

Answer: *the third pig*

What might the words *so that* mean in this sentence? Make three predictions! Choose the meaning that seems to make the most sense.

Answer: *because*

How many short sentences might there be in this long sentence?

Answer: *at least four*

List the four possible sentences.

Answers could be:

1. The third pig built his house out of bricks.

2. The third pig was smarter than the other pigs.

3. The brick house could not be blown down by the wolf.

4. The wolf was hungry.

How to Unravel Complex Sentences That Are in Authentic Texts

Next, students can begin to try to unravel complex sentences in authentic texts. They will try to identify the various simple sentences in a complex sentence and identify what the pronouns stand for. Start with topically and linguistically familiar text materials. Guided reading books at students' levels are good sources of complex sentences. When students begin to master this skill, it will be very apparent. They will beam. They will ask for something harder to figure out.

When they ask for something harder, let them try to understand the ideas embedded in complex sentences in their textbooks, educational magazines, encyclopedias, and online information. Continue to use topics they know about, but make it still harder by having students try to understand complex sentences in adult encyclopedias, newspapers, and journals. Let them try to tease out the individual ideas in some of those monster sentences. If they can begin to do that without flinching, then they have mastered this crucial comprehension strategy.

Teaching Points

♦ Dedicate time to teaching these strategies. It takes students time to learn the various tricks to combining simple sentences into more complex ones. At first, they will learn how to combine two simple sentences in various ways by using commas or pronouns such as *who*, *which*, *that*, and so on. Then you will teach them how to add a third sentence to their complex sentence, then a fourth, and so on until the students have learned how to create 20- to 40-word sentences by employing conventions of print and sentence-combining tricks. Make sure that all your students can create a wide variety of complex sentences with familiar topics before giving them something more challenging.

♦ Use students' lives as topics for complex sentence creation rather than skill-and-drill textbooks or other pre-made materials to teach sentence combining. Do not use language skill textbooks or any commercially prepared skill sheets (either from online sources, workbooks, or textbooks). You can have them write about what happened at the start of the classroom day, or what happened during assembly, or about how to play a computer game that everyone knows. If the students know the topic well, they will be able to decide when their complex sentences make sense, and to what their pronouns refer.

♦ Create sample sentence-combining exercises like those provided in this book. The sample sentence-combining exercises in this book are meant just as a boilerplate for you. Don't use them verbatim. When writing exercises for your own class, make the names of the towns match the students' towns. Change the name of the school to their school's. Use the students' names. Your students will be completely attentive when they see their own names and lives as the subjects of these exercises.

♦ If you tell your students that they will learn how to understand very long sentences as adults do, it will make them happy and eager to try.

♦ When your students seem able to take apart complex sentences about familiar situations, then let them begin to try to understand such sentences about less familiar circumstances. Increase the complexity of the sentences gradually.

♦ The students have to learn how to judge on their own whether or not they have correctly identified all of the embedded ideas. Don't give students hints and clues that are not in the text. Let the text speak for itself.

◆ Show the students how to decide which ideas are embedded in a complex sentence. Guide your students to make multiple predictions about which ideas may be embedded in a complex sentence. Then check to see if each prediction can be supported by the language in the rest of the text. Remind students that if their logical prediction is correct, then it will make sense with subsequent sentences in the paragraph. However, if their prediction is incorrect, it will not make sense with the rest of the context, and they must say, "Good-bye, prediction!"

Frequently Asked Question

I already teach students how to make complex sentences. So shouldn't they automatically understand that they contain several ideas in one sentence?

I have found that my students have not really internalized that complex sentences contain several ideas in one sentence. The first inference they gain through Unraveling Reading Strategy lessons is that the longer the sentence, the more bits of information they can expect to notice in the sentence.

What Is This Sentence Really About?

chapter 9

The Kerneling Reading Strategy

Poor Julia is faced with monster sentences that have many prepositional phrases. She may be able to say all the words, but she is not clear about the gist of the sentence. Julia will very often focus on a phrase and miss the main point. She does not realize she needs to strip away the modifying phrases and hone in on the basic subject, verb, and object of a sentence.

When to Teach the Kerneling Reading Strategy

Kerneling is employed by good readers when they are trying to understand very challenging material such as a sentence in a science textbook. Proficient readers usually attempt to get at the kernel of the idea by mentally scratching out everything except the sentence's subject and verb and direct object. Students are shown how to kernel first with a Kerneling Reading Strategy lesson in which they literally scratch out the modifying words, and then with authentic text that they must read for school but do not understand at all.

Sometimes an author may choose to write an extraordinarily complex sentence with many embedded clauses that modify the subject, verb, and object. Sentences begin to get really complicated by the end of third grade. And it is not unusual for a high school text to have 50, 60, or even 70 words in a single sentence. Remarkably, students are almost never shown how to understand them—not even third or fourth graders. Instead, students are somehow expected to understand these monster sentences on their own, without the benefit of instruction or guidance. They are left to sink or swim by themselves.

Only the most proficient readers know how to deal with a humongous sentence in order to understand it. The purpose of the Kerneling Reading Strategy lesson is to show more advanced readers how to understand at least the gist of lengthy, and seemingly incomprehensible, sentences.

How to Teach the Kerneling Reading Strategy

When faced with a sentence of 50-plus words (a behemoth!), the proficient reader will usually first work to find out the sentence's basic idea. She will endeavor to pluck, from all the verbiage in the sentence, the sentence's subject, verb, and object. I call that type of reading strategy the Kerneling Reading Strategy because the proficient reader is working to determine the kernel of the idea (or the gist of the sentence).

Once the proficient reader gets the basic idea of the sentence, she may then go on to consider the meaning of the many phrases and clauses in that sentence that modify the subject, the verb, and the object. If the reader's prior knowledge of language and concepts is similar to the author's, the reader may be able to sensibly decipher the entire mighty sentence. If the reader's prior knowledge limits her comprehension, then she may only be able to infer the gist of the sentence.

The difference between a proficient reader and someone who is less effective is that the skilled reader will come away with some logical meaning supported by the entire context, while the developing reader may come away with nothing but crossed eyes and a helpless shrug of her shoulders.

Getting Started

Tell students that you have a trick to help them understand very long sentences.

Introduce the idea of prepositions. Supply students with a list of common prepositions and have them read the list aloud a couple of times together to become familiar with them. Here is the list of prepositions I use:

above	beside	in	toward
across	between	into	under
along	by	of	up
around	down	off	upon
at	during	on	with
before	except	over	without
behind	for	through	
below	from	to	

Explain and model the scratching-out procedure.

♦ First, scratch out (~~scratch out~~) all the phrases that begin with prepositions.

♦ Next, scratch out (~~scratch out~~) the remaining words and phrases that don't name but describe people, places, or things (adjectives), or that tell how something is done in a long sentence (adverbs).

♦ The words that remain tell the core idea of the sentence.

Ask students to try it themselves with this sentence:

My enormous brown dog hides under the kitchen table during Florida's hurricane season because he is afraid of thunder and lightning. (21 words)

♦ First, scratch out all the phrases that begin with prepositions:
My enormous brown dog hides ~~under the kitchen table during Florida's hurricane season~~ because he is afraid ~~of thunder and lightning~~.

♦ Next, scratch out all the words that describe a person, place, or thing, or how something is done.
~~My enormous brown~~ dog hides ~~under the kitchen table during Florida's hurricane season~~ because he is afraid ~~of thunder and lightning~~.

♦ This represents a basic understanding of the sentence. It sounds like a headline: Dog hides because he is afraid. (6 words)

Now reverse the process.

Put back all the phrases that you removed to see how the sentence grows longer and longer. As you do this, think about why the author added more words to this sentence to make it longer. Remember, what you are starting with is the main idea of the sentence (*the kernel of the sentence*):

dog hides because he is afraid. (6 words)

♦ First, put back all the phrases that begin with prepositions:
dog hides under the kitchen table during Florida's hurricane season because he is afraid of thunder and lightning.

♦ Next, put back all the words that describe a person, place or thing:
My enormous brown dog hides under the kitchen table during Florida's hurricane season because he is afraid of thunder and lightening. (21 words)

Explore with the students why the author added more words to this sentence to make it longer. Why didn't the author just write a lot of small sentences that say the same thing?

For example, try writing some of the small sentences in this long sentence:

My enormous brown dog hides under the kitchen table during Florida's hurricane season because he is afraid of thunder and lightning. (21 words)

You might come up with a list like this:

1. My dog is enormous.

2. My dog is brown.

3. My dog hides under kitchen tables.

4. My dog hides during hurricane season.

5. My dog hides during Florida's hurricane season.

6. My dog hides because he is afraid.

7. My dog is afraid of thunder and lightning.

Discuss why the students believe the author did not write these seven sentences. If they get stuck, give them some hints. Are the seven sentences interesting to read? Would you like to read an entire story written like this? Why or why not?

Here is another trick to help you understand very long sentences

♦ First, scratch out (~~scratch out~~) all the phrases that begin with prepositions.

♦ Next, scratch out (~~scratch out~~) all phrases that begin with words that function as conjunctions. Here is a list of words and phrases that sometimes function as **conjunctions**:

after	even if	so that	where
although	even though	than	wherever
as	if	that	which
as if	that	though	while
as long as	in order	unless	who
because	or	until	whom
before	since	when	whose
but	so	whenever	

♦ Finally, scratch out (~~scratch out~~) the remaining words and phrases that describe persons, places, or things in the long sentence.

Cross out the phrase introduced by the conjunction in this group of words:
dog hides ~~*because he is afraid*~~.

Here is the ultimate kernel, or the heart of this sentence:
dog hides (2 words)

Here is the original sentence:
My enormous brown dog hides under the kitchen table during Florida's hurricane season because he is afraid of thunder and lightning. (21 words)

Try this with a long sentence from a guided reading book: First reduce the sentence to its kernel. Then, have the kids add back the words and phrases. Let them try to list the various small sentences contained within the long sentence. Do this a few times with fiction and informational text. Then try this with textbook sentences. Start with long sentences that kids understand completely, and then try it with ever longer sentences.

Teaching Points

It seems that most readers who employ this strategy automatically have taught themselves because they want to understand complicated text for their own purposes. They learned through trial and error. Nonetheless, kerneling can be taught.

Three More Types of Kerneling Reading Strategy Lessons

Help your students learn to do these three different, but related, strategies. When they have completed these activities, most will be able to figure out, on their own, the main idea of many extraordinarily complicated sentences. Your students will be able to make sense of much more complicated written language by applying these strategies.

Memorize the Prepositions and Conjunctions

Cross out all prepositional phrases, adverbs, adjectives, and subordinate clauses. What remains is the sentence's subject and verb. Take a lot of time building the students' understanding of how to locate the kernel of a sentence by scratching out phrases and clauses. Make sure the students have memorized the list of prepositions and conjunctions.

A Multiple-Prediction Strategy

Circle the possible subject, verb, and object. See if your choices make sense. Many logical predictions are needed in order to determine the likely kernel of the sentence using this approach. Take a lot of time building the students' understanding of how to locate the kernel of a sentence by logically connecting the subject and verb of the main sentence.

Learn to Create Long Sentences Similar to the Ones Found in Informational Text

Learn to form complex and lengthy sentences using prepositional phrases and subordinate clauses. Start with familiar subjects, everyday language, and very simple sentences. Gradually increase the amount of language to include in one sentence. Start with just one extra phrase. Then add a second phrase. Next, create sentences with two phrases and one subordinate clause. Then add another, and so on.

When teaching students to create their own "monster" sentences, don't go too quickly. Wait until your students have some mastery over just one added phrase before you have them include more in a sentence. Remember, reading research tells us repeatedly that when students know how to build grammatically correct, lengthy, detailed sentences, they will also know how to understand them.

Frequently Asked Questions

1. Do readers really try to root out the heart of a complicated sentence? Don't they just get it without all that scratching-out?

Maybe some students can get this without actually scratching out the modifiers to get at the kernel idea, but not most. It depends on how dense the material is. I employ this drastic strategy when I am forced to read a document containing 50-, 60-, or even 80-word sentences. Certainly, I would not choose to read such material, but it happens often enough as I seek out information for one purpose or another.

2. Will students really remember all the prepositions and all the conjunctions?

Not usually. When I teach this strategy, I put the list of prepositions near every student and I also put them on the footer of every strategy lesson page. Likewise, when I am highlighting conjunctions, I put those words on the footer of every page and on a sheet of paper for every student. With time, students remember a lot of them, especially the older students. By the way, this particular trick was extremely helpful to ELL learners who needed a way to get to the kernel idea in complex sentences. My ELL learners willingly memorized all the prepositions and all the conjunctions so they could find the main ideas contained within this type of sentence.

Conclusion

Are You Ready to Fly?

So, there you have it. Once you understand the reading strategies employed by proficient readers and a variety of ways to present them to developing readers through Reading Strategy lessons, you have a repertoire of options that can be applied, as needed, with any student who is struggling with reading comprehension—irrespective of age, irrespective of subject matter. My hope is that this book demonstrates such an approach. However, once you truly understand the reading strategies and how to share them, you can and should improvise variations on my approach. Remember, although the strategies are presented in a sequence that seems to work well for most students, there is no strict order to teaching them. With a little time and experience using them, you will be able to recognize which of the basic strategies applies in each situation and you will be able to support and challenge your learners appropriately.

Here is my mantra for you: Have fun teaching the reading strategy lessons to your students! It is easy to do since the learners really love them. Remember to let the students figure out as much as they can for themselves through their use of logic, prior knowledge, knowledge of English, and their all-important belief that written language should make sense. You are ready to fly!

Appendices: Reproducibles

I n order to help you apply the strategy lessons described in our book, I have prepared some lessons that you can reproduce and use with your students in your classroom. In order to save paper, when the lessons are brief, the lessons are printed two on a page. The directions for implementing the lessons are included in the text. Have fun!

Name _____ Date _____

2/1 Cloze Reading Strategy Lesson

Example #1 is paired with Example #2. In each case, the reader is shown the sentences gradually until the entire story is revealed. Keep the last sentence hidden, then reveal it after all the guessing has simmered down.

Example 1

I am not happy. My _____ is broken. Now I can't

_____ because it won't _____. My mother said

someone will come to fix it tomorrow. I hope so. I like to _____ when

I get home. I am a big baseball and basketball fan! I love to watch the Yankees and the

Nets when they are playing.

Example 2

I am not happy. My _____ is broken. Now I can't

_____ because it won't _____. My mother said

someone will come to fix it tomorrow. I hope so. I like to _____ it

when I get home. I like to peddle around the park.

2/2 Cloze Reading Strategy Lesson

One-Sentence Cloze With Blanks

1. There is _____ candy in the bag for everyone.

2. I raise my _____ when I want my teacher to call on me.

3. The football fan _____-ed, "My team is the best!"

4. I have a _____ on my face and it hurts.

5. My father is _____-ing tonight's meal. I hope it tastes good.

6. I looked _____ in my brand new suit.

7. I _____ the pizza as fast as I could.

8. Today I _____-ed my room. It smells so nice now.

9. I needed a match to_____ the fire.

10. My baby brother cries _____-ly. I wish he would stop crying.

11. The big bad bully tried to _____ me.

12. The _____ from my brother's room could be heard in every room of the house.

13. The mother _____, "Don't fight with your sister!"

14. I have a _____ bag of popcorn for the movies.

15. The medicine helped to _____ my stomach ache.

Name _____ Date _____

One-Sentence Cloze With Blanks

16. If you don't spend your allowance for a few months, you might be able to _____ a lot of money.

17. The fans at a basketball game are _____ when their team scores a basket.

18. The scary movie I saw made me feel _____.

19. The balloon _____ into the sky.

20. I had a party to _____ my birthday.

21. At the end of the school day, many parents _____ outside the school in order to pick up their children.

22. On Halloween, I was _____-ed to look like a witch.

23. I worked _____ on my project, and I got an "A" from the teacher.

24. The price for the computer was _____ , so I did not buy it.

25. I have colorful hair clips _____ to my braids.

26. This book is too hard to _____!

27. A girl asked her mother, "Would you put some milk in my _____?"

28. I am lost because I cannot _____ the nurse's office.

29. At my birthday party, the kids _____-ed in my backyard.

2/3 Cloze Reading Strategy Lesson

One-Sentence Cloze Containing an Unfamiliar Word

1. There is ample candy in the bag for everyone.

2. I raise my appendage when I want my teacher to call on me.

3. The football fan bellowed, "My team is the best!"

4. I have a blemish on my face and it hurts.

5. My father is concocting tonight's meal. I hope it tastes good.

6. I looked dapper in my brand new suit.

7. I devoured the pizza as fast as I could.

8. Today I sanitized my room. It smells so nice now.

9. I needed a match to ignite the fire.

10. My baby brother cries incessantly. I wish he would stop crying.

11. The big bad bully tried to menace me.

12. The reverberations from my brother's room could be heard in every room of the house.

13. The mother scolded, "Don't fight with your sister!'

14. I have a voluminous bag of popcorn for the movies.

15. The medicine helped to alleviate my stomach ache.

One-Sentence Cloze Containing an Unfamiliar Word

16. If you don't spend your allowance for a few months, you might be able to amass a lot of money.

17. The fans at a basketball game are animated when their team scores a basket.

18. The scary movie I saw made me feel anxious.

19. The balloon ascended into the sky.

20. I had a party to commemorate my birthday.

21. At the end of the school day, many parents congregate outside the school in order to pick up their children.

22. On Halloween, I was costumed to look like a witch.

23. I worked diligently on my project, and I got an "A" from the teacher.

24. The price for the computer was exorbitant, so I did not buy it.

25. I have colorful hair clips fastened to my braids.

26. This book is too hard to fathom!

27. A girl asked her mother, "Would you put some milk in my goblet?"

28. I am lost because I cannot pinpoint the nurse's office.

29. At my birthday party, the kids romped in my backyard.

Here is a very simple Cloze Reading Strategy lesson that highlights the idea that once the reader gets the gist of the writing, she can assign logical meaning to several words that are unfamiliar to her within the text. In this case, the reader is faced with four unfamiliar words represented by blanks.

Name _____ Date _____

2/4 Cloze Reading Strategy Lesson

Jane was late for class again! When she got into the school building,

Jane _____ up the stairs. Then Jane _____ down the hall.

She _____ the classroom door and _____ into her seat.

Another form of Cloze Strategy Reading lesson is to have words alien to most students in familiar contexts. The students are invited to take logical guesses at the meaning of the sentences, and the unknown words. Then they look up the unknown words in *The Clear and Simple Thesaurus Dictionary* by Wittles, Greisman and Morris (1996) to see how smart they are.

Name _____ Date _____

2/5 Cloze Reading Strategy Lesson

Example 1

This week, I commemorated Halloween. Children romped from door to door, entreating adults for confections. Some children appeared as ghouls, goblins, skeletons, and witches. Others were costumed as doctors, astronauts, or teachers. Children adore this holiday.

Name _____ Date _____

2/6 Cloze Reading Strategy Lesson

Now let the children apply the Cloze Reading Strategy with authentic text. Photocopy a page that they are trying to understand. Let the children work in pairs to first identify the words they do not recognize, then decide what the sentences containing those words might mean. Then ask the pair to assign a useful synonym or phrase for the word(s) and, if possible, to identify the word itself by asking themselves (Mantra) "What could this be that means *this* and looks like *that*?"

Ask the reader to assign a function to each proper noun in fiction. Follow procedure outlined on page 32.

Name _____ Date _____

Histmanitnlaoria and The Bistominstao Sweet Shoppe

By Simiotminoanintianotnekondoanei Reinsod

Histmanitnlaoria was a little, grey, furry dog. He was lost and could not find his way home. He was looking in town for his owner.

Histmanitnlaoria passed by the bakery called The Bistominstao Sweet Shoppe. Ms. Bistominstao saw the dog and came outside. She said, "Hi, Histmanitnlaoria! I am glad to see you. Your owner, Mr. Rishtonema, is looking for you. Stay here and eat a cookie."

Ms. Bistominstao kept Histmanitnlaoria inside The Bistominstao's Sweet Shoppe until Mr. Rishtonema showed up. Mr. Rishtonema was so happy to have Histmanitnlaoria back!

Answers:

H probably is _____

The B probably is _____

Ms. B probably is _____

Mr. R probably is _____

Ask the reader to assign a function to each proper noun in informational text, then follow the procedure outlined on page 32.

Name _____ Date _____

The Topie and Jestimono Story

Topie was sad that Jestimono could not come to her birthday party in Moeno. "Why can't you come?" wailed Topie. Jestimono loved his teenaged granddaughter and wanted to see her, but Jestimono had to be one thousand miles away from Moeno for his work.

Jestimono was working in Riroperpempg creating computer programs. But Jestimono had an idea! On the day Topie celebrates her fourteenth birthday, they would both use their Sooneoins to see and speak to each other. It would be just like Jestimono was at Topie's party.

Topie in Moeno was able to hear Jestimono sing "Happy Birthday" to her from Riroperpempg. Aren't computers great!

Person, place, or thing?

What kind of person, place, or thing?

1. Topie is probably _____

2. Jestimono is probably _____

3. Moeno is probably _____

4. Sooneoin is probably _____

5. Riroperpermgp is probably _____

Ask the reader to assign a function to each proper noun in informational text.

Name _____ Date _____

3/3 Nicknaming Reading Strategy Lesson

In 2530 Cimonono Created Beosnoer.

In 2530 Cimonono created the Beosnoer in the country of Troeonoonoqwnm. It made it possible for children to eat as much candy as they like without getting sick—ever. President Stieonon gave Cimonono the Rankfrhlpingchirenetmrechoclatel Award for her invention of the Beosnoer which made every child happy in Troeonoonoqwnm.

Hint: In the story, circle the first letter of each proper noun so you can see the names better.

1. C is probably (a person? a place? or a thing?)
    What kind of person or place or thing? What did it do?

2. B is probably (a person? a place? or a thing?)
    What kind of person or place or thing? What did it do?

3. T is probably (a person? a place? or a thing?)
    What kind of person or place or thing? What did it do?

4. S is probably (a person? a place? or a thing?)
    What kind of person or place or thing? What did it do?

5. R is probably (a person? a place? or a thing?)
    What kind of person or place or thing? What did it do?

Now I Get It! © 2010 by Joan Lazar and Christine Vogel: Scholastic Professional

3/4 Nicknaming Reading Strategy Lesson

From: *Origins of the Dinosaurs*
by Steve Parker Grolier Educational, 0-7172-9406-4, p. 36

Eoraptor was probably in the subgroup of sauischians known as the theropods. The theropods included all meat-eating dinosaurs, from tiny Compsognathus to the great Allosaurus and Tyrannosaurs. The Eoraptor lived during the Late Triassic Period—about 200 million years ago. Staurikosaurus was probably slightly larger than the Eoraptor, which was the size of a small dog. The Staurikosaurus' thighbone was angled sideways to fit into the acetabulum. This gave the Staurikosaurus the ability to stand up straight.

Answer the question, and underline the information that supports your answer.

1. Is E a theropod or a Late Triassic Period? E is a _____

2. Who was bigger E or Sta? _____

3. What might be special about theropods? _____

4. Name three possible theropods: _____

5. What might an acetabulum be? _____

6. What might the Late Triassic Period mean? _____

7. What could the Sta do that was special for dinosaurs? _____

I working with Scattered Clues Reading Strategy lessons it is important not to show all the clues at once. The journey is what is important. Directions for implementing these powerful lessons begin on page 43.

Name _____ Date _____

4/1 Scattered Clues Reading Strategy Lesson

My family and I went to _____.

We went on Saturday.

We got on line early to get good seats.

When the lights went out, the picture came on.

4/2 Scattered Clues Reading Strategy Lesson

My family and I went to _____.

We went on Saturday.

We got on line early to get good seats.

Present various final clues to see how the meaning of the first sentence changes.

- I loved seeing the New York Knicks shoot baskets.

- Why didn't the Giants win the game?

- It was exciting because there were so many people singing on the stage.

- When the lights went out, the picture came on.

4/3 Scattered Clues Reading Strategy Lesson

I want to go to _____.

I hope there is a short line for tickets.

Present various final clues to see how the meaning of the first sentence changes.

- I hate to sit too close to the screen.

- Behind "home plate" is the best place to sit.

- I hope I can see the actors on stage.

4/4 Scattered Clues Reading Strategy Lesson

Sara lost her _____.

They had been in her pocket.

Now she cannot get inside her house.

Present various final clues to see how the meaning of the first sentence changes.

- Now she cannot see well.

- Now she cannot drive to work.

- How will she pay for the groceries?

4/5 Scattered Clues Reading Strategy Lesson

Last night I had _____.

I did not want to eat.

Today I feel better.

The dentist fixed it.

4/6 Scattered Clues Reading Strategy Lesson

June took her brother's _____.

He was happy about it.

June told him to say, "Cheese," and to smile.

4/7 Scattered Clues Reading Strategy Lesson

I do not want to _____.

It tastes awful.

I have do it every single night,

so that I will not have many cavities.

4/8 Scattered Clues Reading Strategy Lesson

I am in _____ very often

except when it rains.

No one is allowed to go in during a storm.

The life guards say that lightening can harm swimmers.

4/9 Scattered Clues Reading Strategy Lesson

I won _____.

I can't take it outside in the winter time.

So I will put it in a warm place in my room.

I will give it a lot of water.

When Spring comes, I will plant it in my backyard.

I hope the petals will be bright red, and the stems will not have too many thorns.

The Blixer

The blixer was blixing in the smetnen. It was very helpful.

The blixer was rospented in 1806.

1. Where was the blixer blixing?

    a. in the smetnen

    b. in the broster

2. When was the blixer rospented?

    a. in 2006

    b. in 1806

3. Is the blixer

    a. a good thing. Why?

    b. a bad thing. Why?

The Meldot and the Bonpel

Both the Meldot and the Bonpel complent. They exuset by the desanin.
However, only the Meldot can exuset without a toolel.

1.   What do the Meldot and the Bonpel do the same?

    a. toolel

    b. complent

2.   What is different about the Meldot?

    a. The complent

    b. It can exuset without a toolel.

3.   Does the Bonpel probably need a toolel to exuset?

    a. Yes. Why?

    b. No. Why?

Now I Get It! © 2010 by Joan Lazar and Christine Vogel: Scholastic Professional

Many Types of Eee

Many types of eee can make hhh, including xxx, yyy, and zzz. Only xxx uses the sun to make hhh. Both yyy and zzz use water. Not every kind of eee can make hhh. For example, ttt cannot because it does not have rrr.

Directions: Write your answer to each question below the question.

1. Which types of eee can make hhh?

2. What are the two ways to make hhh?

3. How are yyy and zzz similar?

4. How are xxx and yyy different?

5. Which type of eee cannot make hhh?

6. What does ttt need in order to be able to make hhh?

7. On the back of this page, explain what you paid attention to the most to answer these questions.

Name _____ Date _____

Types of Bbb

The rrr and the ccc are similar kinds of Bbbs. An rrr is taller and lighter than a ccc. An rrr never drinks water. It eats fruit instead. A ccc can't eat fruit, because fruit gives it too much gas.

Directions: Write your answer below the question.

1. How many types of Bbbs are there? What are their names?

2. Which Bbb would you rather lift up if you had to? Why?

3. Which Bbb would probably drink water? How do you know?

4. Which Bbb would you not like to be around if it eats fruit?

 Now I Get It! © 2010 by Joan Lazar and Christine Vogel: Scholastic Professional

Unravel this sentence containing *who*.

Directions: There are at least two ideas in this sentence. List two possible sentences that can be made from this one sentence.

Ms. Lazar, *who* reads a book every evening, is teaching us how to read better.

Answers could be:

1. _____

2. _____

8/2 Unraveling Reading Strategy Lesson

Directions: There are at least two ideas in this sentence. List two possible sentences that can be made from this one sentence

Ms. Novolilski, *who* is a fourth grade teacher, teaches at Setimbit School.

Answers could be:

1. _____

2. _____

Directions: There are at least three ideas in this sentence. List three possible sentences that can be made from this one sentence.

The big hungry wolf blew down the house and ate the pig who had made a house of straw.

Answers could be:

1. _____

2. _____

3. _____

Directions: There are at least three ideas in this sentence about the pigs. List three possible sentences that can be made from this one sentence.

The third pig, who was smarter than the other pigs, built his house out of bricks, which stopped the wolf from blowing it down.

Answers could be:

1. _____

2. _____

3. _____

There are at least two ideas in this sentence. List two possible sentences that can be made from this one sentence.

Ms. Lazar read to us *The Littles*, which is an interesting book.

Answers could be:

1. _____

2. _____

Now I Get It! © 2010 by Joan Lazar and Christine Vogel: Scholastic Professional

Name _____ Date _____

Directions: There are at least two ideas in this sentence. List two sentences that can be made from this sentence:

The two pigs were lazy so they made hay or straw houses, which blew down easily.

Answers could be:

1. _____

2. _____

Name _____ Date _____

How are long sentences made?

This long sentence was made with the word *who* and with two commas.

Ms. Lazar, who teaches reading to the fourth grade, is going on vacation. (13 words)

1. What could the word *who* mean in this sentence? Make three predictions! Choose the meaning that seems to make the most sense.

   ANSWER _____

   _____

   _____

2. How many short sentences might there be in this long sentence?

   ANSWER _____

3. What are possible sentences?

   ANSWER _____

   _____

   _____

Now I Get It! © 2010 by Joan Lazar and Christine Vogel: Scholastic Professional

How are long sentences made?

This long sentence was made with the word *who* and with two commas.

Ms. Jewel, who is our fifth grade teacher at Thurgood Marshall School, is reading a book to us. (18 words)

1. What could the word *who* mean in this sentence? (Hint: Make three predictions! Then choose the meaning that seems to make the most sense.)

   ANSWER _____

   _____

   _____

2. How many short sentences can you see in this long sentence?

   ANSWER _____

3. Write some of the possible sentences below.

How are long sentences made?

This long sentence was made with the words *that, and, who.*

The big hungry wolf blew down the house that was made of straw and ate the pig who was hiding inside. (21 words)

1. What could the word *who* mean in this sentence? (Hint: Make three predictions! Choose the meaning that seems to make the most sense.)

    ANSWER _____

    _____

2. What could the word *that* mean in this sentence? (Hint: Make three predictions! Choose the meaning that seems to make the more sense.)

    ANSWER _____

    _____

3. How many short sentences can you make from this long sentence?
    ANSWER _____

    On the back of this page, list the possible sentences.

Now I Get It! © 2010 by Joan Lazar and Christine Vogel: Scholastic Professional

How are long sentences made?

This long sentence was made with the words *who*, *so that*, and two commas.

The third pig, who was smarter than the other pigs, built his house out of bricks so that the hungry wolf could not blow it down. (26 words)

1. What could the word *who* mean in this sentence? (Hint: Make three predictions! Choose the meaning that seems to make the most sense.)

    ANSWER _____

    _____

2. What might the words *so that* mean in this sentence? (Hint: Make three predictions! Choose the meaning that seems to make the most sense.)

    ANSWER _____

    _____

3. How many short sentences can you find in this long sentence?

    ANSWER _____

    On the back of this page, list four possible sentences.

8/11 Unraveling Reading Strategy Lesson

This long sentence was made with the use of *that, they, their, which, when,* and *them.*

The two pigs were so lazy that they made their houses quickly with hay or straw which fell down very easily when the hungry wolf blew on them. (28 words)

1. What could the word *they* mean in this sentence? (Hint: Make three predictions! Choose the meaning that seems to make the most sense.)

   ANSWER _____

   _____

2. What could the word *which* mean in this sentence? (Hint: Make three predictions! Choose the meaning that seems to make the most sense.)

   ANSWER _____

   _____

3. How many short sentences can you find in this long sentence?

   ANSWER _____

   On the back of this page, list four possible sentences:

Now I Get It! © 2010 by Joan Lazar and Christine Vogel: Scholastic Professional

How are long sentences made?

This long sentence was made with the words *which*, *who* and two commas.

Ms. Lazar read to us an exciting book entitled, *The Littles*, which told about small mice-like people who have adventures. (21 words)

1. What could the word *who* mean? (Hint: Make three predictions and pick the meaning that seems to make the most sense.)

    ANSWER _____

    _____

2. What could the word *which* mean? (Hint: Make three predictions and pick the meaning that seems to make the most sense.)

    ANSWER _____

    _____

3. How many short sentences can you find in this long sentence?

    ANSWER _____

    On the back of this page, list at least four sentences that can be made.

8/13 Unraveling Reading Strategy Lesson

Create a long sentence yourself using the word *who*.

Now you make a long sentence from a bunch of short sentences about Cinderella. Use the word *who* to connect the sentences.

A.   Combine these two sentences using the word *who*.

   1. The fairy tale is about Cinderella.

   2. Cinderella is a young girl.

One long sentence: _____

_____

_____

_____

Now I Get It! © 2010 by Joan Lazar and Christine Vogel: Scholastic Professional

8/14 Unraveling Reading Strategy Lesson

Create a long sentence yourself using the word *who*.

Now you make a long sentence from a bunch of short sentences about Cinderella.

B.   Combine these two sentences using the word *who*.

1. Cinderella lives with her stepmother and two stepsisters.

2. The stepmother is cruel and nasty.

One long sentence: _____

_____

_____

8/15 Unraveling Reading Strategy Lesson

Create a long sentence yourself by using the word *which*.

Now you make a long sentence from a bunch of short sentences about Cinderella.

C.   Combine these two sentences using the word *which*.

1. Cinderella had to do all the cleaning and washing for the family.

2. Cinderella hated doing all the cleaning and washing for the family.

One long sentence: _____

_____

_____

8/16 Unraveling Reading Strategy Lesson

Create a long sentence yourself by using the words like *that, but,* and *which.*
Now you make a long sentence from a bunch of short sentences about Cinderella.

D.   Combine these three sentences. Hint: Words like *that, but,* and *which* might help
     you to combine these sentences together into one long sentence.

   1.   The Prince was having a party to meet the young ladies in the town.

   2.   Cinderella's family was going to the party.

   3.   Cinderella was not allowed to go to the party.

One long sentence is: _____

_____

8/17 Unraveling Reading Strategy Lesson

Create a long sentence yourself by using words like *who, that, but,* and *which.*
Now you make a long sentence from a bunch of short sentences about Cinderella.

E.   Combine these three sentences. Hint: Words like *who, that, but,* and *which* might
     help you to combine these sentences together into one long sentence.

   1.   Cinderella had only dirty old clothes to wear.

   2.   A fairy godmother helped Cinderella go to the party.

   3.   The fairy godmother made Cinderella a beautiful gown.

One long sentence might be: _____

(continued on the back of the page)

Now I Get It! © 2010 by Joan Lazar and Christine Vogel: Scholastic Professional

8/18 Unraveling Reading Strategy Lesson

Create a long sentence yourself by using words like *who, that, but, because* and *which.* Now you make a long sentence from a bunch of short sentences about Cinderella.

F.   Combine these three sentences. Hint: Words like *who, that, but, because* and *which* might help you to combine these sentences together into one long sentence.

    1. Cinderella had to leave the party at midnight.

    2. Cinderella danced with the Prince.

    3. Cinderella ran out of the Ball at midnight.

    4. Cinderella left her glass shoe at the party.

One long sentence might be: _____

_____

_____

Create a long sentence yourself by using words like *who, that, but, because* and *which*. Now you make a long sentence from a bunch of short sentences about Cinderella.

G.   Combine these three sentences. Hint: Words like *who, that, but, because* and *which* might help you to combine these sentences together into one long sentence.

1. The Prince looked for Cinderella all over the town.

2. The Prince asked all the women to try on Cinderella's glass shoe.

3. Finally, the Prince found Cinderella.

4. Cinderella's foot fit into the glass shoe.

5. The Prince and Cinderella married.

One long complex sentence might be:

_____

_____

_____

_____

8/20 Unraveling Reading Strategy Lesson

Unravel these long sentences.

Cinderella's Godmother changed the girl's rags into a beautiful gown, her mice into horses, and her pumpkin into a coach.

1. _____

2. _____

3. _____

4. _____

8/21 Unraveling Reading Strategy Lesson

Unravel this long sentence that was made with commas.

When the clock struck midnight, Cinderella ran out of the castle, leaving her slipper behind.

1. _____

2. _____

3. _____

Summarize Cinderella in five sentences.

Try to summarize the Cinderella story in no more than five sentences by using sentence combining tricks you have learned. You have written three sentences so far. Good Work!

1. Cinderella had to do the chores for her family and she couldn't go to the Ball.

2. Cinderella had a fairy godmother who made Cinderella's carriage, fancy clothes and glass slippers so she could go to the Ball.

3. Cinderella met the Prince at the Ball but she ran away and left her glass slipper behind because the spell was about to wear off at midnight.

Now you write two more long sentences to finish the story. Make sure you tell only the most important information. Remember to use any tricks you need to combine ideas such as the words: *who*, *which*, or *that*, as well as commas and pronouns. Write your two final sentences here:

4. _____

_____

5. _____

_____

Now I Get It! © 2010 by Joan Lazar and Christine Vogel: Scholastic Professional

Mantra 2/1

The Goal of Reading

Whenever I read anything, I try to understand what it is about.

Mantra 2/2

Ask yourself, "What could this mean that would make sense to me?" Then tell yourself, " Make three predictions!"

Mantra 4/1

Say "Goodbye" to predictions that no longer make sense.

Mantra 5/1

If you can say it accurately in your own words, you understand it.

Mantra 8/1

One long sentence can be broken down into several smaller sentences.

References

Altwerger, B. (Ed.). (2007). *Rereading fluency: Process, practice, and policy*. Portsmouth, NH: Heinemann.

Atwell, N. (2007). *The reading zone: How to help kids become skilled, passionate, habitual, critical readers*. New York: Scholastic.

Beaver, J. (2004). *Developmental reading assessment*. Lebanon, IN: Celebration Press, Pearson Learning Group.

Boran, S., & Comber, B. (Eds.). (2001). *Critiquing whole language and classroom inquiry*. Urbana, IL: National Council of Teachers of English.

Cowhey, M. (2006). *Black ants and Buddhists: Thinking critically and teaching differently in the primary grades*. Portland, ME: Stenhouse.

Fletcher, R. (2006). *Boy writers: Reclaiming their voices*. Portland, ME: Stenhouse.

Flurkey, A. D., & Xu, J. (Eds.). (2003). *On the revolution of reading: The selected writings of Kenneth S. Goodman*. Portsmouth, NH: Heinemann.

Flurkey, A. D., Paulson E. J., & Goodman, K. S. (Eds.). (2008). *Scientific realism in studies of reading*. New York, NY: Lawrence Erlbaum Associates.

Goodman, D. (1999). *The reading detective club: Solving the mysteries of reading. A teacher's guide*. Portsmouth, NH: Heinemann.

Goodman, K. (1967). Reading: A psycholinguistic guessing game. *Journal of Reading Specialist*, 6, 126–135.

Goodman, K. (1996). *On reading: A common-sense look at the nature of language and the science of reading*. Portsmouth, NH: Heinemann.

Goodman, Y. M., & Burke, C. L. (1972). *Reading miscue inventory manual: Procedure for diagnosis and evaluation*. Katonah, NY: Richard C. Owen Publishers, Inc.

Goodman, Y. M., & Burke, C. L. (1980). *Reading strategies: Focus on comprehension*. New York: Holt, Rinehart and Winston.

Goodman, Y. M., & Marek, A. M. (1996). *Retrospective miscue analysis: Revaluing readers and reading*. Katonah, NY: Richard C. Owen Publishers.

Goodman, Y. M., Watson, D. J., & Burke, C. L. (1996). *Reading strategies: Focus on comprehension* (2nd ed.). Katonah, NY: Richard C. Owen Publishers.

Halpern, J. (1998). *A look at snakes*. Austin, TX: Steck-Vaughn.

Harvey, S., & Goudvis, A. (2000). *Strategies that work: Teaching comprehension to enhance understanding*. Portland, ME: Stenhouse.

Harvey, S., & Goudvis, A. (2005). *The comprehension toolkit: Language and lessons for active literacy*. Portsmouth, NH: Heinemann.

Hoyt, L. (2002). *Make it real: Strategies for success with informational text*. Portsmouth, NH: Heinemann.

Johnson, P. (2006). *One child at a time: Making the most of your time with struggling readers, K–6*. Portland, ME: Stenhouse.

Keene, E. O., & Zimmerman, S. (1997). *Mosaic of thought: Teaching comprehension in a reader's workshop*. Portsmouth, NH: Heinemann.

Macdonald, Wendy. (2000). *Training a guide dog*. Barrington, IL: Rigby.

Miller, D. (2002). *Reading with meaning: Teaching comprehension in the primary grades*. Portland, ME: Stenhouse.

Mills, H., O'Keefe, T., & Jennings, L. B. (2004). *Looking closely and listening carefully: Learning literacy through inquiry*. Urbana, IL: National Council of Teachers of English.

Mooney, M. E. (2004). *A book is a present: Selecting text for intentional teaching*. Katonah, NY: Richard C. Owen, Publishers.

Parker, D. (2007). *Planning for inquiry: It's not an oxymoron!* Urbana, IL: National Council of Teachers of English.

Parker, S. (2000). *The age of the dinosaurs*. Danbury, CT: Grolier.

Schoenbach, R., Greenleaf, C., Cziko, C., & Hurwitz, L. (1999). *Reading for understanding: A guide to improving reading in middle and high school classrooms*. San Francisco, CA: Jossey-Bass.

Short, K. G., Harste, J. C., with Burke, C. L. (1996). *Creating classrooms for authors and inquirers*. Portsmouth, NH: Heinemann.

Smith, F. (1971). *Understanding reading: A psycholinguistic analysis of reading and learning to read*. New York, NY: Holt, Rinehart and Winston, Inc.

Smith, F. (1978). *Reading without nonsense*. New York: Teachers College Press.

Smith, F. (2007). *Reading FAQ: Expert answers to frequently asked questions*. New York, NY: Teachers College Press.

Smith, R. K., & Goldstein, J. M. (1993). *English brushup*. Marlton, NJ: Townsend Press.

Tatum, A. (2005). *Teaching reading to black adolescent males: Closing the achievement gap*. Portland, ME: Stenhouse.

Wilde, S. (2000). *Miscue analysis made easy*. Portsmouth, NH: Heinemann.

Wittels, H., & Greisman, J. (1996). *The clear and simple thesaurus dictionary*. New York: Grosset & Dunlap.